Samuel Johnson

Purgatory Prov'd by Miracles

collected out of Roman-Catholick authors - with some remarkable

histories relating to British, English, and Irish saints - with a preface

concerning the miracles

Samuel Johnson

Purgatory Prov'd by Miracles
*collected out of Roman-Catholick authors - with some remarkable histories relating
to British, English, and Irish saints - with a preface concerning the miracles*

ISBN/EAN: 9783337361228

Printed in Europe, USA, Canada, Australia, Japan

Cover: Foto ©Lupo / pixelio.de

More available books at **www.hansebooks.com**

Purgatory Prov'd

BY

MIRACLES:

Collected out of

Roman-Catholick Authors.

With some Remarkable

HISTORIES

Relating to

British, English, and Irish Saints.

With a Preface concerning the Miracles.

No Article was ever with more force of Spirit, or more grave Authority set forth since the beginning of Christian Religion, than this one of Purgatory; never Nation was Converted to the Faith, but had this Truth not only Taught by Word, but by Miracles also Confirmed. W. Allen's Defence of the Catholick Doctrine of Purgatory, p. 112.

LONDON:

THE
PREFACE.

READER,

THIS Collection of Miracles was intended as an Appendix to the School of the Eucharist, and to let the Hereticks know further, that if the Papists please they can trump up Miracles to prove all their other Doctrines, as well as that single one of Transubstantiation. Nay, they have out-done their own Business in that kind, for they have employed Miracles against one another, to prove the contrary Points of Doctrine which are amongst themselves: So that the World has not only been filled with Roman Catholick, but, for instance, with Dominican and Franciscan Miracles. For to pass by the Tragedy of Jetzer which is of elder date, it is well known how the Pullets Eggs in the Canaries have been of late years both Maculists and Immaculists, and have been found in quite contrary Stories. For when the Franciscans were baffled in their other Arguments, they betook themselves to this last and most unanswerable Method of Confuting their Adversaries, and accordingly one of them brings an Egg to the Bishop of the Canaries, which was well attested to be found in a Pullet's Nest, with an Inscription of Letters which seemed to grow in the Shell of it, That the Virgin Mary was Conceived without Original Sin. This Miracle stunnied the Dominicans for some time; but always set a Priest to catch a Priest, for by that time the Dominicans were Virtuoso's sufficient to prepare one, They also had a Pullet's Egg out of the Nest with the quite contrary Inscription upon it: And if the Bishop had not put a stop to these Proceedings, no body knows where their Miracles would have ended. The Truth of this Story is so well known to the English Merchants who have of late been in the Canaries, that for the substance of it I will refer my self to the Spanish Walk upon the Exchange, and I am sure I have not willingly varied in any Circumstance.

The PREFACE.

But will any man of common Sense call such Forgeries, as all these are, by the Sacred Name of Miracles? Or entitle the little Cheats of Priests to the Almighty Power of God? No surely; for not only every Christian has a surer Word of Prophecy to give heed unto, but also every Natural Man has a better Light to guide him, than to be imposed upon by Lying Wonders. For as for Christians, it is a first Principle with them, That if an Angel from Heaven teach any other Gospel than what they have received from Christ and his Apostles, that Angel is a false and accursed Spirit, and not to be believed; And with mere Natural Men it is an undoubted Axiom, That God cannot deny himself, nor work any Miracle which is Inconsistent with his own Divine Nature: So that if any pretended Miracles to attest such Doctrines as are contrary to the plain and express revelation of Scripture, and to the unchangeable Nature of God, we are able at the first sight, both as Men and Christians, to pronounce such Miracles to be false and counterfeit. Upon both of these accounts we are sure that the School of the Eucharist is an heap of Forgeries, which are not fit to be endured either by Men or Christians. For the Doctrine of Transubstantiation, in behalf of which God is said to have wrought all those amazing Miracles, is expresly contrary to Scripture, which teaches us, That Christ's Body is a true Humane Body, in Humane Shape and Proportions: Whereas Transubstantiation quite contrary makes no more but a little Breaden Apparition of the self same Body, and will force us to believe, That it is in the form of a Crumb of Bread. Again, all Miracles wrought in behalf of Transubstantiation, are wrought to Prove, That both the sides of an infinite number of Contradictions are True; But as we are men we are infallibly certain, that it is Impossible for both sides of a Contradiction to be True: From whence we are alike certain, That it is Impossible for the God of Truth to set his Seal to Transubstantiation, that is to say, to such a number of Falshoods.

The same may be shown in the other Points of Popery, as Invocation of Saints and Angels, Worship of Images, Worship of Relicks, or Dead Mens Bones, Prayers in an Unknown Tongue, &c. which are downright Contradictions both to the Doctrine of Scripture, as also to the Principles of Natural Light, and the everlasting Notions which we have of God. But because Purgatory *is the matter which lies before us, I shall chuse rather to instance in that.*

Trid. Ca-
tech. Sub
Artic.
Symbol.
descendit
ad Inferos
Sect. 5. And 1. The Popish Doctrine which says, That amongst the Receptacles or Apartments of Hell, there is a Purgatory-fire wherewith the Souls of the Godly being tormented for a limited time are cleansed from Sin, that so they may have a passage into their Eternal Country into which no unclean thing shall enter, is plain

b y

another Gospel; for I challenge all the World to shew me where our Saviour or his Apostles have Preached any such Gospel: Nay, it is a contrary Gospel, for it stands in a direct and diametrical opposition to the principal Doctrines of Christianity, as has been largely and learnedly shewn by Dr. Sherlock in The Second Part of his Preservative against Popery. So that if the Papists had fourty times more Miracles than they have for the establishment of Purgatory, yet while we are Christians we must reject both it and them as Forgeries and Falshoods.

2. As we are men we are able to shew the falshood of that Doctrine, and consequently of all the Miracles wrought in behalf of it. For let men call an old Heathenish Poetical Fiction by the Name of an Article of the Catholick Faith, the new Name does not alter the nature of the Thing, nor make a Fiction to be a Truth.

I shall therefore examine Purgatory as a Doctrine of the Poets, but by no means as a Doctrine of Christianity, and consider what a wise Heathen would have said to it. And 1. He would say, That to suppose the Souls of the Godly to be an unclean Thing, is a contradiction in terms; for an unclean Soul is an ungodly Soul. 2. He would say, That Fire is no means of purging away the Defilements of a Soul, nor can a spiritual substance be chymically prepared for Heaven. 3. He would make work with their contradictious Charity in Praying for Souls out of Purgatory, in giving Alms and saying Masses to help them out, when yet they stedfastly believe with a Divine Faith, that those Souls were sent thither on purpose for their good, and that if the punishments of Purgatory be not necessary for their entrance into Heaven, they went thither in vain. 4. Though he were a very Philosopher, he would smile as much, to think how one man's Alms or Aves should supply the place of a purging Fire and refine another man's dross, as he would to think how one man's taking Physick should make another man Well. In short, he would think of this Doctrine, and of all the Miracles which support it, as he ought to think.

This is a sure way of judging concerning all other Popish Miracles, even of the great Xavier's, which the Author of the Pulpit Sayings, p. 21. brags to have gained credit amongst Protestants themselves. But for certain those Protestants had never read Xavier's Persic Gospel, translated as I remember by Ludovicus de Dieu, for then they must have concluded, that God would never give his Letters of Credence to such a false Apostle, nor employ his own Almighty Power to gain belief to such an heap of Falshoods as there is, yea though they be mixed with some Truths, for the Devil himself never spoke all Lies.

B.

The PREFACE.

It is easie to apply this Rule, which can never fail, to all the Miracles in this following Collection, which are such as cannot be reconciled with Christianity, nor the natural Notions which we have of God. God and Nature do nothing in vain; But can any thing be more vain and sportive than those Matches of Miracles, which we have p. 32 and 44? Where Omnipotency is employed to less purpose, than the Capping of Verses betwixt two School-boys, or than if one of them should stand to blow out a Candle, while the other blew it in again. And if those Miracles which passed betwixt St. Molva and St. Modoc, p. 44. have any meaning at all, they tend only to confirm the Doctrine of Abstaining from Meats; which Doctrine has but a very bad Character, 1 Tim. 4. 3. and therefore those Miracles are undoubted Impostures. For the Doctrines of Devils shall never be confirmed with God's Miracles.

But every Reader is able to judge for himself, which of these Miracles are to no purpose, and which are for the Priest's purpose, and to make the Popish Pot boyl, as the Fire of Purgatory plainly is; which are for the honour of the Saint, and the dishonour of God; which are fit to enslave men's minds, and which are fit to widen their Belief, that they may the more easily swallow the Mysteries of Popery; and in a word, which of them serve best for those Superstitious and Antichristian Uses, which the Church of Rome knows very well how to put them to. And therefore I shall only take notice of one single Miracle, but it was a Breeder and had a great many more in the belly of it, and that is the Staff of Jesus, which Justus the Hermite was ordered to deliver to St. Patrick, of which you have an Account p. 42, 43. Now I only ask, Whether the Christians said their Creed that Morning, when Jesus Christ had lain all Night at Justus's Cell, and when he delivered to him the Staff? For at that time either the Article of his sitting in Heaven, or else his delivering of the Staff, and ascending afterwards into Heaven, was not true. And I desire some Romish Priest to tell me which it was.

𝔓urgatory 𝔓rov'd
BY
MIRACLES:
Collected out of
Roman-Catholick Authors.

The History of a Man, that having experienc'd the Pains of Purgatory, chose much rather to suffer the Miseries of Humane Life, for many Years together, than Three Days Torments in Purgatory.

WE read in St. *Antonin*, that a Man who had been extremely debauch'd, was visited by God with a long and painful Sickness. As he was a great lover of his Pleasure, and his Distemper putting him as it were upon the rack, he at length lost all Patience, and earnestly besought our Lord, that he would send Death to him. An Angel appeared to him, that offered him the choice, either to continue sick as he was two Years longer, or spend three Days in Purgatory. This Man being only sensible of his present pain, preferr'd three Days in Purgatory, before a two Years sickness. But hardly had he been an Hour in those Dreadful Flames, but that the same Angel came to visit him there, and askt him in what condition he found himself. Ah! he answer'd, you have deceiv'd me; For I was to have been but three Days in Purgatory, and whereas I have now been several Years here. No, the Angel retorted, I have not deceived you. But it is the violence of your pains, that makes you think the little time you have been here so long. Ah! for God's sake, reply'd he, do so as that I may again return into life; For I am ready to suffer all the pains of my Distemper, not only during two Years, but as long as it shall please God to afflict and punish me. He obtain'd what he required, and never after did he complain of the pains he endured. *Le Pedag. Christien*, p. 508.

How

How a certain Holy Person was induc'd to Pray for Souls in Purgatory.

A Holy Man, call'd *Bertrand*, a Provincial of the Order of St. *Dominique*, said Mass daily for the expiation of his own sins, without troubling himself with offering it to God for the repose of Souls in Purgatory. Being one day askt the reason of this, he answer'd, That those Souls were secur'd of their salvation, and by consequence, that they had less need of Prayers than the living. The Night following a dead man appeared ten times to him, knocking his hand against his Coffin, and making a shew as if he would maul him. Which possess'd him with so great a fear, that he rose up betimes in the Morning, and went to say Mass for the Dead ; and all the rest of his Life he spent in procuring by all sorts of means their ease and delivery. *Pedag. Chrest.* p. 512.

The Account of a Man in Purgatory, for neglecting to Pray for the Dead.

IN the Year 1541. a holy religious Priest, of the Order of St. *Francis*, appeared after his Death to a Novice, who pray'd for him, and told he was in Purgatory, because he had been negligent in praying for the Dead. *Pedag. Chrest.* p. 513.

A Virgin, after having been in Purgatory, and Heaven itself, returns upon Earth, for the good and Conversion of Sinners.

ST. *Christina*, a Virgin, and Native of St. *Thron* in *Hasbaye*, being dead, her Soul was convey'd into a place, where they suffer'd such horrible torments, that she thought it to be Hell ; but an Angel assur'd her, that it was only Purgatory. From thence she was carried into Heaven before the Throne of God, who left it to her choice, whether she would remain eternally with the Blessed in glory, or be re-united to her Body, to labour for the deliverance of those Souls which she had seen suffer such dreadful Punishments, and afterwards return into Heaven, there to receive the Crown which she had merited by her good Works. She took this last course, and at the same instant she re-entred into her Body, which was laid publickly at that time in the midst of the Church, while they were saying Mass. From that time this Saint perform'd such rigorous Penances, and such amazing Mortifications, that she justly acquired the Sir-name of *Admirable*. *Le Pedag. Chrest.* p. 513. The

The Thanks of the Dead, for the Prayers of the Living.

ST. *Liebert*, Bishop of *Cambray*, one day praying in *St. Nicholas's* Church-yard, in the same City, for those that were there enterr'd, and with great devotion saying this Verse, which the Church so often sings: May the Souls of all the Faithful that are Dead rest in Peace.; a Voice was heard in the Air, that answer'd chearfully and distinctly, So be it. *Le Ped. Chrest.* p. 514.

A Person that devoted his Whole Life for the Redemption of the Dead.

JEan *Ximenes*, of the Company of *Jesus*, a religious Man of extraordi-nary Vertue, praying for the Dead on the day of *All Saints*, before the Image of the Immaculate Conception of our Lady, heard a Voice that said to him, *Ximenes, remember you the Souls that are in Purgatory.* Which so sensibly affected him, that he offer'd to God for them all his Morti-fications, all his Good Works, and generally all the Acts of Vertue, whether Interior, or Exterior, that he was to do from that time till death. *Le Pedag. Chrest.* p. 515.

St. Thomas Aquinas his Purgatory Expeditions.

ST. *Thomas Aquinas*, saith the Reverend Father *Ribadeneyra*, in his *Flowers of the Lives of Saints*, was wont to demand three things of Almighty God with great Instance: The first was force to serve him without ever relenting in that first Primitive fervour wherewith he had undertaken his service. The second, that he would be pleased to keep him always in the humble and poor condition of a Religi-ous state, which he had made profession of. And the third was, that he would reveal unto him, what state his Brother *Arnold* was in, whom the Emperour *Conrade* had put to death, because he stuck to the Party of the Church. All which three things our Lord granted him in ample manner. For he gave him Grace to persevere in his service until death in his Religious Order, with great sanctity ; and he revealed unto him in a Vision, that his Brother was in the state of Salvation; our Lord recompencing the Death which he was put unto for his Service and for the Defence of the Church. His Sister, that had taken a Religious Course, appeared once unto him, whilst he was praying, and told him, that she was in Purgatory, demanding the Assistance of his Sacrifices and other Prayers. The Saint was very careful to help her with Masses, Fastings, Prayers,

B 2   both

both by himſelf and by other Religious Men. And few days after, ſhe appeared again for to thank him for the benefit he had procured unto her, for that ſhe was now in Glory. *St. Thomas* asked her, of the condition of his two Brothers, and of his own ſtate, *Whether it were good in the preſence of God ?* She anſwered, *That their Brother* Landulſfe *was in Purgatory, and* Arnold *was at reſt ; and that for what concerned himſelf, he was in the Grace of God, and that ſhortly they ſhould all of them meet together, but he ſhould be far higher in glory, for his good Service and Pains taken in the Church.* Moreover, at another time, when he was one Night praying in the Church of his Convent, at *Naples,* Fryar *Romanus,* who ſucceeded him in the Chair of Divinity in *France,* being lately deceaſed, appeared unto him, *St. Thomas* having yet underſtood nothing of his death ; after that he knew him, and was told by him, that he was departed out of this World, he inquired of him, *Whether his Services were acceptable unto God, and if he were in the ſtate of Grace?* *Romanus* bid him, *go on and perſevere in the ſtate he was in, for it was very good, and God was well pleaſed with it.* Then *St. Thomas* asked *Romanus, how all things went with him, and where he was ?* To whom he replied, *that he was now in Heaven ; but had been fifteen days in Purgatory for a neglect which he had committed in the Execution of the Biſhop of* Paris *his Will, in a Matter which ought to have been performed out of hand, and was delayed by his fault.* Some other things did *St. Thomas* ask him, and was ſatisfi'd in them all, after which *Romanus* vaniſhed; leaving him in great comfort and conſolation. For when God will reveal ſome ſecrets unto his ſervants, he uſeth firſt to give them a Deſire, and moveth them by his Holy Inſpirations for to demand them of him, giving them an aſſured confidence of obtaining what they ask : upon which Ground they walk ſecurely, which they could not do, if that Divine Motion were wanting, and if through a vain curioſity they did pretend to know the ſecret Judgments of our Lord, and the ſtate of Souls departed out of this Life: as many times it falleth out. *Fat. Peter Ribadeneyra's* Flowers of the Lives of the Saints, *p. 204.*

Whence came the Cuſtom of ſaying Thirty Maſſes for the Dead, which are called the Maſſes of St. Gregory.

ST. *Gregory* the great Pope and Doctor, came to underſtand that a certain Monk that was ſick, and ready to die, had hoarded up three hundred Crowns. This ſeemed unto him to be ſo grievous an offence, that he commanded the Prior of the Monaſtery, whoſe name was *Precioſus,* to ſee that none of the Religious ſhould viſit him, or af-

Flowers of the Lives of the Saints, n.223.

ford him any Comfort ; to the end that seeing himself thus neglected by all, he might at least in that Extremity, acknowledge his Fault, do Penance, and come to be saved. The poor man died, and the Saint would not permit his Body to be buried with the rest, but to be cast upon a Dunghil, together with his three hundred Crowns : and all the Monks said, *Pecunia Tua tecum sit in Perditionem*; *Thy Money perish with thee.* This Rigor was very profitable: for when the Proprietory Monk perceived that all abhorred him, he had great feeling of his Crime, and died penitent: and the rest, that they might not incur the like Punishment, laid at the Abbots feet all they had, even those things which they might keep according to the Rule. After thirty days, the holy Father taking compassion of the Soul of this poor man, commanded *Preciosus* to say Mass for him every day for thirty days consequently ; at the end whereof the deceased Monk appeared to a Brother of his, that was a Religious Man, and told him, *That he had been in Purgatory until that day, but that now by the mercy of God he was going to Glory.* And this was the effect of the thirty Masses which St. *Gregory* commanded to be said for him. Whence came the custom of saying thirty Masses for the Dead ; which are called, *The Masses of Saint Gregory.*

St. Stanislaus *Bishop and Martyr, raises up a Man to life that had been three years dead, to be his Witness in a Process he had depending.*

THE Reverend Father *Ribadeneyra*, in his said *Flowers of the Lives of the Saints*, does acquaint us in the Life of St. *Stanislaus* Bishop and Martyr, how that that holy Bishop had bought, for the benefit of his Church, a piece of Land of a Rich man named *Peter*, and had faithfully paid him the price of it ; but yet could not shew sufficient Evidences for the proof of the same. The man that sold him this Land had now been dead three years: And his Heirs, for to please the King, who bore a great enmity to the Saint, and to make their benefit of so fair an occasion, complained of the Bishop in a Juridical Court, that he had seized upon an Inheritance that belonged to them. The Business was brought to be examined before the King ; who finding that the Bishop wanted some necessary Writings, and that the Witnesses, for fear of his displeasure, durst not inform the Court of the Truth, condemned him to restore the Lands to *Peter's* Heirs, as due and proper to them by right of Inheritance. The Saint demanded three days for to bring *Peter* before them, of whom he had bought the Land, and who, as we said, had been dead and buried three years be-

The Flowers of the Lives of the Saints, p. 324.

fore. They easily granted him his demand; making a jest and sport of it. But the Saint fasted, watcht and pray'd with great fervour and instancy, begging of our Lord, *That seeing the Cause was his, and that it was he who was wronged and injured by that unjust Sentence, be would be pleased to take the whole Business in hand, and rise up in his own defence.* At the end of three days, having offered up the Holy Sacrifice of Mass, he went unto the Grave where *Peter* lay buried, and made the Grave-stone be taken away, and the Earth opened until the Body appeared : Then touching the said Body with his Crosier-staff, commanded *Peter* to rise. At which instant the dead Body obeying the Voice of the living Saint, *Peter* rose up and followed him to the Court, where the King was, accompanied with all his Nobles and Judges. To whom *St. Stanislaus* spoke thus : *Look here is Peter, of whom I bought the Land ; who having been dead, is risen again, and now standeth before you. Ask of him if it be true that I paid him entirely that for which he sold and I bought that Land for the Church. The man is sufficiently known, his Grave is open : It is God who raised him to life, for the confirmation and assured proof of this Verity. His Word ought to be a more certain and infallible Argument of it, than all the Testimony of Witnesses, or Evidence of Writings that can be alledged.* This so great and manifest a Miracle did extreamly daunt the Courage of the Bishop's Adversaries, and struck them to the very heart, so that they remained quite dumb, and had not one word to say : For *Peter* declared publickly the Truth, and very gravely and seriously warned his Heirs *to do Penance for this their sin, and for having so much molested the holy Prelate, contrary to all Equity and Justice.* St. *Stanislaus* offered *Peter*, if he desired to remain some years in Life, to obtain it for him of Almighty God. But he chose rather to return to his Grave, and die again presently, than to abide in so troublesome and dangerous a Life : and told the Saint, *That he was in Purgatory, and that yet he had something to suffer in satisfaction for the remnant of his sins : and that he had rather be secure of his salvation, although it were by undergoing the rest of the pain and torment due to his former sins, than engage himself in the hazard and jeopardy, by embarking anew to be tossed in the stormy and tempestuous Sea of this wicked World. That he begged of him to beseech our Lord to remit and pardon him the rest of his Punishment, and to release him soon out of that Prison, and bring him to enjoy his glory in the blessed company of Saints.* When he had said this, St. *Stanislaus* accompanied him to the Grave, and a multitude of people went along with them. *Peter* laid himself down in his Tomb, and composed himself for his last Rest ; and begging of all the Assembly for to recommend his Soul unto our Lord, died the second time, for to go to live eternally with Almighty God.

St. Teresa *by her Prayers rescues a Person out of Purgatory.*

A Certain Gentleman, who had given the Saint (viz. *Teresa*) an *The Flow-* Inheritance for the founding of a Monaftery in *Valliodolid*, not *ers of the* long after fuddenly fell fick and died, and his Speech failing him, he *Lives of the Saints,* was not able to make a full Confeffion, although he gave great figns of *p. 793.* Contrition. She hearing of his Death, was much afflicted for him, fearing left perhaps his Soul was damned ; and as she was recommen-ding him to God, our Lord told her, That his falvation had been in great danger, and that he had shewed him mercy for the fervice he had done his Mother, giving her a House for the building of a Monaftery there of her Order, and that he should come out of Purgatory when the firft Mafs should be faid there, and not before. The Saint having heard this, being fo full of Charity as she was, for that she had always before her Eyes the grievous pains that this Soul endured, could find no repofe until she had founded the Monaftery. And to the end that we might know of the compaffion that our Lord has of the Souls that are in Purgatory, and how pleafing and gratefnl that is unto him, which is done for them, himfelf one day, feeing that the Saint, by rea-fon of certain Affairs which occurred, made fome delay to go to *Vallio-dolid* to found the faid Monaftery, haftened her on as she was in Pray-er, bidding her to make haft away, for that that Soul fuffered much. And all was fulfilled as had been revealed unto her: for Mafs being ended, and the Saint approaching to receive the Holy Communion, the Gen-tleman who had been Mafter of the House and Garden, where she and her Companions now were, appeared unto her with a glorious and chearful countenance, and thanked her with joyned hands for that which she had done for his delivery out of Purgatory ; and after this he mounted up to Heaven.

A Vifion of Purgatory, Hell, and Paradife.

A Certain Husbandman, called *Thurcillus*, living at *Tidftude* a Vil- *Matt. Pa-* lage in the Bifhoprick of *London*, a perfon very Hofpitable to his *ris, F. 181.* capacity, while he was in his Field, *Julianus* the Hofpitator appeared to him, bidding him be ready at night, when he would call upon him, there being matters to be divinely shew'd him, that were beyond the apprehenfions of Humanity. Accordingly he came; and bidding *Thurcillus* to leave his Body to reft in his Bed, for that his Soul was only to troop along with him.

Coming to about the middle of the World, they entred into a glo-rious

rious Court that had a wonderful light arifing, faid the Guide, from the decimation of the Juft. Here they met with St. *James*, who had fent for this Stranger, and he bid St. *Julian* and St. *Domnius*, the Keepers of the place, fhew the Stranger the penal places of the Wicked, and the Manfions of the Juft. Hereupon St. *Julian* inform'd him that this was the Court for all Souls newly departed their Bodies; and there the Places and Manfions were forted and affign'd as well for the damn'd, as for thofe that were to undergo the torments of Purgatory. This place was conftituted by our Saviour upon the Interceffion of the glorious Virgin *Mary*, for the reception of Souls that are new born in Chrift, that they may there convene as foon as they leave the Body, to be try'd according to their Works, without any invafion of the Devils. And this is call'd the Congregation of Souls. The Souls of the Juft were perfectly white, and had the Afpects of Youths. Without this Wall was the place of punifhment for thofe that us'd injuftice in matter of Tythes, and the Saint perceiving by our Strangers coughing in paffing by it, that he had been tardy in that bufinefs, he commanded him to make a publick Confeffion of it at his return before the whole Congregation, and require Abfolution from the Prieft.

Eaftwardly between two Walls, was a vaft place of Purgatory-fire, and beyond it a Pond to renfe Souls in that had waded through Purgatory, the water being falt and cold beyond comparifon. Over this Purgatory St. *Nicholas* was the Overfeer.

There was a mighty Bridge all befet with Nails and Spikes, and leading to the Mount of Joy: On which Mount was a ftately Church, feemingly capable to contain all the Inhabitants of the World, and into which the Souls were no fooner entred, but that they forgot all their former torments.

Returning to the firft Church, there they found St. *Michael* the Archangel, and the Apoftles *Peter* and *Paul*. St. *Michael* caus'd all the white Souls to pafs through the Flames, unharm'd, to the Mount of Joy; and thofe that had black and white fpots, St. *Peter* led into Purgatory to be purified.

In one part fate St. *Paul*, and the Devil oppofite to him with his Guards, with a pair of Scales between them, weighing all fuch Souls as were all over black; when upon weighing a Soul the Scale turn'd toward St. *Paul*, he fent it to Purgatory there to expiate its fting; when towards the Devil, his Crew with great triumph plung'd it into the flaming Pit.

Now it happened one Evening that they faw a Devil coming full fpeed upon a black Horfe, whom his Companions went out to meet with great triumph. St. *Domnius* forc'd the Fiend to tell him whofe
Soul

foul it was he fo racked with riding. He anfwered, That it was a Peer of *England*, who di'd the night before, without Confeffion, or receiving our Lord's Body: That he had render'd his People very miferable upon the inftigation of his Wife; and that having turn'd him into that Horfe-like form, he had brought him down to eternal punifhment. And then the Fiend cafting his Eyes upon the Ruftick, *Who's he*, quoth he to the Saint? Quoth the Saint, *Doft not know him?* faid the Fiend, *I faw this man at* Tidftude *Church in* Effex *at the time of its Dedication.* Cry'd the Saint, *How went you in?* To whom the Fiend anfwer'd, *In a Woman's Garb; by the fame token that coming up to the Font, and meaning to go into the Chancel, the Deacon met me with a holy Water-ftick, and fo frighted me with the fprinkling of that Water, that giving a fkream, I leapt at once two furlongs from the Church into a Field.* And the Ruftick did affirm, that he and others had heard the noife, but were altogether ignorant of the meaning.

Then the Ruftick, under the protection of the Saints, faw the Devils Stage Plays: Firft, they introduc'd a proud man in his Robes, ftrutting along big, cocking his Eye-brows, uttering fwelling Words, in fhort having all the manners of Imperioufnefs and Arrogancy; but while he was threatning horrible Executions, and priding himfelf in his Trappings, all on the fudden they turn'd into a flame about him, burning him moft difmally, and then the Devils feizing him, tormented him beyond what humane Malice can imagine.

Then entred a Prieft, whofe Tongue they toar out, and then made him fuffer the fame torments as the proud man, for not having given his Flock either Exoftation, or a pious Example, or Prayers, or Maffes, for the temporal Goods he received from it.

Then came a Souldier arm'd *Cap-a-pee,* and mounted on a black Horfe, prauncing and brandifhing his Spear againft the Devils, and boafting of his Exploits; but after fome play, they difmount him, and he had the fame fate as the former.

Then they introduc'd a Lawyer, the moft famous of all *England*, but ended his life miferably in the very year of this Vifion. He was wont to take Fees on both fides, and the Fiends now forc'd him to act the fame over again: for he admit'd here on the right and left, and took

Then came an Adulterer and an Adulteress, reprefenting the very act of Copulation, with the moft filthy venerial motions, and immodeft poftures, before the whole Affembly. And then becoming as it were diftracted, they fell bitterly upon one another, changing their fuperficial Love into Cruelty and Hatred. And then were by the Infernals, in like manner as the former, as alfo all Fornicators are, with punifhments beyond defcription.

Then two Backbiters enter'd with wry faces and odd grimaces. The two heads of a burning Spear were put into their mouths; which knawing upon with diftorted looks they quickly met at the middle, and then tearing one another, they all embru'd their faces with biting.

Then Thieves, Incendiaries, and Violators of holy places, were introduc'd, and were rack'd by the Devils upon burning Wheels, and fundry other Inftruments of torment.

The Ruftick likewife faw near the entrance of the lower Hall as it were four Streets; the firft was full of innumerable Furnaces and Cauldrons fill'd with flaming Pitch & otherLiquids, and boiling of fouls, whofe heads were like thofe of black Fifhes in the feething Liquor. The fecond had its Gauldrons ftor'd with Snow and Ice, to torment fouls with horrid Cold. The third had thereof boiling Sulphur and other materials affording the worft of ftinks for the vexing of fouls that had wallow'd in the filth of Luft. The fourth had Cauldrons of a moft horrid falt and black Water. Now finners of all forts were alternately tormented in thefe Cauldrons.

Now returning to the Temple, upon the Mount of Joy, the Ruftick had a fight of the introduction of pure white fouls, and was made fenfible how much they were help'd to the poffeffion of eternal Joys, by the means of the Maffes of their Friends in the World : nay, and faw many of his Acquaintance dancing Attendance upon *St. Michael* for admittance. That Saint likewife fhew'd him the feveral Manfions and Apartments of thofe that gradually mounted up to infinite Happinefs; and how they at certain hours each day heard Canticles from Heaven, as if all the forts of Mufick in the World had joyn'd in confort.

Then he led him to a place all bedeckt with infinite variety of Flow-

denotes the joy he receives from the ineffable glorification of his Sons that are to be faved; and by the other weeping one, denounces the forrow he undergoes on the account of the rebrobation of fome of his Sons, and the juſt Judgment of God upon the damned. The Veſt-ment with which he is covered, but not a compleat Robe, is the Veſt of Immortality and Glory, which he was ſtript of at his firſt prevari-cation: for he began to receive this Veſt from *Abel* his juſt Son, till now thro' the whole ſucceſſion of his juſt Sons. And as the Eleĉt ſhine with various Virtues, ſo this Veſt is piĉtured of a various colour. When the number of the Eleĉt Sons ſhall be compleat, then *Adam* ſhall be all o-ver cloath'd with a Robe of Immortality and Glory; and ſo the World ſhall be at an end.

Then the Saint led the Ruſtick into a much more raviſhing place than any yet feen, and there ſhew'd him *St. Catharina, St. Margareta,* and *St. Oſitha,* whoſe beauty having admired, *St. Michael* bid *St. Julian* con-vey him back to his Body, and accordingly did ſo, but how is not known. He lay as it were in a Trance for two days and two nights after, but after that repairing to Church, he was follicited by the Prieſt and his Pariſhoners to acquaint them with his Revelations; but he de-clining ſo to do, *St. Julian* appear'd to him the night following, and commanded him to gratifie them in that point. And in obedience to the Saint, he gave an account of his Viſion in the *Engliſh* Tongue, with ſuch Eloquence as created admiration in all his Auditors; and the more as having been known to have ever been a man of narrow ſence and few words.

The occaſion of the Inſtitution of a ſet and ſolemn day, for the Praying for Souls out of Purgatory.

THE Cardinal *Peter Damian,* a very holy and very learned man, writes in the Life of *St. Odilo* Abbot of *Cluny,* (who died in the year of our Lord 1048) that a Religious man of *France* returning from *Hieruſalem,* was by a Tempeſt carried to an Iſland or Rock, where there was an holy Hermite, who told him that there hard by were great burn- The Flow-ers of the Lives of the Saints, p. 828.

to change him in his name to persevere in that holy Exercise, and by his fervent Prayers and continual Alms, to endeavour to give refreshment to the souls of our Brethren that are tormented in Purgatory, that so the joy of the Blessed might be increased in Heaven, and the sorrow of the Devils in Hell. The Religious man returned into *France*, communicated that which he had heard of the holy Hermite with *Odilo* Abbot, and with all that blessed Congregation which was under his charge : And the Abbot ordained that in all his Monasteries, upon the second of *November*, the day after the Festivity of *All Saints*, should be made a particular Commemoration of the Dead, and that especial care should be used to succour and relieve them, by Prayers, Alms, and Masses. And that which St. *Odilo* instituted in his Convents, was afterwards received and established by Apostolical Authority in the whole Universal Church. *Peter Galesinus* Protonotary Apostolical, says, that many write, that Pope *John* XVI. instituted this Commemoration by the counsel and advice of St. *Odilo*. It is true, that *Almarius Fortunatus* Bishop of *Trevers*, who lived about 200 years before *Odilo*, in a Book of the Ecclesiastical Offices, which he wrote to *Ludovicus Pius* Emperour, after the Office of the Saints, he puts that of the Dead ; and he says that he did so, because many depart out of this Life, who do not go presently to Heaven, for whom that Office was wont to be said : which is a sign that even in his time this was done, as Cardinal *Baronius* has noted. And this is sufficient to declare the Institution of this Commemoration of the Dead, and the occasion of making of it.

Certain Revelations which the Saints have had concerning the Souls in Purgatory.

Flowers of the Lives of the Saints, p. 830. St. *Gregory* the Great writes, that the Soul of *Paschasius* appeared to St. *German*, and testified unto him, that he was freed from the pains of Purgatory for his Prayers. When the same St. *Gregory* was Abbot of his Monastery, a Monk of his, called *Justus*, now dead, appeared to another Monk, called *Copiosus*, and advertized him, that he had been freed from the Torments of Purgatory, by thirty Masses, which *Pretiosus*, Prefect of the Monastery by the Order of St. *Gregory*, had said for his Soul, as is recounted in his Life. St. *Gregory* of *Tours* writes of a Holy Damzel, called *Vitaliana*, that she appeared to St. *Martin*, and told him, that she had been in Purgatory for a venial sin which she had committed, and that she was delivered by the Prayers of the Saint. *Peter Damian* writes, that St. *Severin* appeared to a Clergy-man, and told him, that he had been in Purgatory, for not having said the Divine Service at due hours, and that afterwards God had

had delivered him, and carried him to the company of the blessed.
St. Bernard writes, that *St. Malachy* freed his Sister from the pains of
Purgatory by his Prayers, and that the same Sister had appeared unto
him, begging of him that relief and favour. And *St. Bernard* himself
by his Intercession freed another, who had suffered a whole Year the
pains of Purgatory : as *William Abbot* writes in his Life. And *St. Rembert*, Archbishop of *Bremes*, fasting forty days for a Priest, called *Arnolfus*, freed him out of Purgatory : and the same *Arnolfus* appeared
to him, and gave him thanks for it, as *Surius* relates in his Life. And
St. Thomas of *Aquin*, being at his Prayers, a sister of his, a religious
woman, now dead, appeared unto him, and told him, how that she
was in Purgatory : and afterwards she appeared to him again, giving
him thanks for the benefit, which by the means of his Fasts, Prayers,
and Masses, she had received, and for the glory which she now had in
Heaven. *Pope Benedict* the Eighth, being now dead, appeared to
St. Odilo Abbot, (of whom we spoke before) glorious and beautiful,
and gave him thanks, with profound reverence, confessing, that by
his Prayers, and the Prayers of his Religious, God had done him the
favour to take him out of the prison of Purgatory, and to place him
in Heaven amongst the Elect.

St. Martin *raises one from the Dead.*

WIthout the City of *Poictiers*, St. *Martin* built a poor Monastery
for himself and for some of those that followed him. Amongst
these was one, a *Catechumen*, who, when St. *Martin* was upon a time
out of the Convent, fell sick of such a violent Disease, that within a
few days it took away his life, and he died without being baptized.
The Saint returned home, and found his Monks much afflicted, for
what had hapned; and the Corpse of the dead Man, ready to be carried
to the Grave : He approached near unto him, sad and disconsolate :
looked stedfastly upon him with great feeling, and by a particular
impulse from God, commanded them all to go out of the Chamber,
and the Doors being shut, stretched himself upon the cold Body of
the Dead Man, and making a fervorous Prayer to our Lord, besought
him to restore him to life : and our Lord did so, insomuch that those
who were without, expecting the event, entring into the Chamber,
to their great admiration and astonishment, found him alive, whom
they were about to bury. The *Catechumen* they revived, received
immediately the Water of Holy Baptism, and lived many years,
and recounted how that his Soul being gone out of the Body, was presented before the Tribunal of God, and that it was condemned to be

Flowers of the Lives of the Saints, P. 856.

in certain obscure and dark places, but that presently after it understood by the Angels, that *St. Martin* prayed for it, and that the Judge had commanded them to carry it back to the Body, and to present it as from him to his Servant *St. Martin.*

Of Fishermen that fish up a Soul in a Piece of Ice.

* Part 4. Sum Major: tit. 14. ca. 10. de Septemp. Purg. Sect. 7.

THe Author of Purgatories, *Knell,* relateth from * *Antoninus* of certain Fishermen, who drawing their Net to Land, found therein a massy piece of Ice, whereof they were not a little glad, because they knew it would be a welcom Present to *Theobald* their Bishop, who was exceedingly tormented with a burning heat in his Feet ; Neither were they deceived, for it stood him in great stead. One day amongst the rest, as he was cooling his Gouty Toe, he heard a Voice from out of the Ice, whereupon he conjures it to tell, who or what it was. The Voice answers, *I am a Soul afflicted for my sins in this Ice, and unless you say thirty Masses for me, thirty whole days together, I shall not be delivered.* *Theobald* instantly betakes him to his Beads, and begins his task. Whilest he was at his work, there is News brought of an Army approaching to sack the Town. The Bishop is driven to give over his Devotion for that time. When the Hurly-burly was past, he falls to his Bus'ness the second time, but with as ill success ; for then there arose a Civil Commotion in the Town. The third time he means to make all sure: but see, (as the Devil would have it) the whole City, with the Bishop's Palace, was all on a light fire ; his Servants were importunate with him, to cast away his Book, and to provide for his own safety. Do what they could, they could not prevail. All the Answer they could get is this, that though the Town should be burnt to the ground, he is resolved not to give over, till he had made an end. To be short, he was as good as his word. Would you hear the issue? He had no sooner finished, but the Ice melted, the Soul was delivered; and the Fire vanished ; neither was there any damage at all received. If this be not true, ask the Fishermen ; Poor Souls, they little thought they had taken such a Booty.

The Choice of a Soul in Purgatory.

* Sermones discipuli de tempore, & de sanctis promptuario exemplorum, in the 160 Serm. of the Souls.

A Certain * Author writes, that there was a Soul which had lain 20 Years in Purgatory, and at last there came an Angel, who did bid the Soul chuse, whether it would tarry yet one short Winter's day in Purgatory, or that it would return into the World again, and there do a marvellous hard Penance, to wit, for one long hundred Years

Years fpace, fhould go bare-foot, and tread ftill upon fharp Iron Nails, eat nothing elfe but brown Bread, and drink bitter Gall, mingled with Vinegar, and wear a Cloth of Camel's Hair next the Skin, and a Stone under the Head, in place of a Pillow. This Soul did chufe much rather to do all that fame hard Penance on Earth, than to tarry one day longer in Purgatory.

Of the miraculous Efficacy of Alms and Prayers for Souls departed, in an Inftance of their Extending to the Living when miftakingly applied

THe Author of *the Defence of Purgatory, and of Prayer for the Souls De- parted,* recounteth as from *Bede* in this his old *English;* how that in a fighten Field betwixt *Egfride* and *Edeldred,* two Princies of our Land, it fortuned that a yonge Gentleman of *Egfrides* Army, fhould be fo grievoufly wounded, that falling down both himfelf without fenfe, and in all mens fights, ftark dead, he was letten lye of the Ene-mies, and his Body fought with care to be buried of his Friends. A Brother of his, a good Prieft and Abbot, with diligence making fearch for his Body, amongft many happened on one that was exceeding like him, (as a man may eafily be deceived in the alteration that ftreight falleth upon the Soul's departure, to the whole form and fafhion of the Body) and beftowed of his Love, the duty of Obfequies, with folemn Memorials for the reft of him, whom he took to be his Brother decea-fed: burying him in his pwn Monaftery, and caufing Mafs to be done daily for his pardon, and Soul's releafe. But fo it fortuned, that his Brother *Huma,*(for fo was he caulled) being not all-out dead, within four and twenty Hours came reafonably to himfelf again : and gathering withal fome ftrength, rofe up, wafht himfelf, and made means to come to fome friend or acquaintance, where he might falve his Sores, and clofe his Woundes again : But by lacke of ftrengthe to make fhifte, and by misfortune, he fel into his Enemies handes: and therby the Capi-taine examined of his Eftate, he denied himfelf to be of Name or De-grie in his Coontry. Yet by the lykelyhoods that they gathered of his coomly demeanure, and Gentleman-lyke taulke, which he could hardly diffemble, they miftrufte (as it was indeede) that he was a Man of Arms, and more than a Commen Souldear. Therfore in hope of good gaine by his raunfon, they thought good after he was full recovered, for fear of his efcape to lay Irons upon him, and fo to make fure-work. But fo God wrought, that no fetters could howld him : For every day once at a certaine houre, the bandes bracke lowfe without force, and the man made free. The Gentleman marvailed at the cafe himfelf, but his

Of Prayer for Souls Departed, p. 211.

kepers and the capitaine were much more aftoyned thereat, and ftraite-
ly examined him by what cooning or crafte he could with fuch eafe
fet himfelf at libertie : and bare him in hande, that he ufed Characters
or Letters of fum forcery and whichcrafte, with the practife of unlaw-
full artes. But he anfwered in fadneffe, that-he was alltogether unskil-
ful in fuche thinges. Mary (quod he) I have a brother in my coontry
that is a prieft, and I knowne certainly, that he faithe often Mafs for
my foule, fuppofing me to be departed and flaine in batayle, and
if I were in an Other Lyfe, I perceive my foul by his interceffion
fhould be fo lowfed out of paines, as my body is now from bondes :
The capitaine perceiving fo much,and belyke in fum awe of Religion,
feeinge the worke of God to be fo ftraunge, fould him to a *Londoner* ;
with whome the fame things happened in his bondes lowfing every day.
By which occafion he was licenfed to go home to his friends,and procure
his ranfom, for chargeing him with divers forts of fureft bands, none
could fallfely howlde him. And fo upon promiffe of his returne or pay-
ment of his appointed Price, he went his wayes, and afterward truely
difcharged his Credit.Which doone by friendfhip that he fownd in the
fame Coontry, afterward returned to his owne parties, and to his brother's howfe : to whome when he had uttered all the Hiftory of his
ftraunge fortune,both of his mifery and miraculous relieving,he enquired
diligentlye the whole circumftance,with the howre and time of his daily
lowfinge,and by conferring together,they fownde that his bondes brake
lowfe, efpecially at the very jufte time of his celebration for his foule.
At which times he confeffed, that he was otherwife in his great adver-
fities often releafed alfo. Thus hath that holy Writer allmoft word
for word, and att thende he addeth this : *Many bearing thus much of the
Party himfelf,were wonderfully inflamed with faith and zeale,to pray, to give
almefe, and to offer facrifice of the holy Oblation, for the delivery of theire wel-
beloved frendes departed out of this life. For they underftood, that the health-
full facrifice, was availeable for the redemption of both Body and Soule everlaft-
ingly. And this ftorie, did they that heard it of the Parties owne Monthe, re-
ported unto me. Whereupon having fo good proofe,I dare be bowlde to write it
in my Ecclefiaftical Hiftory.* And thus much faithe *Beda* abowte eghte-hun-
dred yeares ago, when our Nation being but yonge in Chriftianity,was
fedde in the true Belief, by fundry wonderous Workes of God.

*Allin's Defence and Declaration of the Catho-
lick Churches Doctrine of Purgatory,* p. 211.
Printed at Antwerp, by John Latius*,
with Priviledge,* 1565.

St. Catherine *of* Sienna's *Vision of a Soul in Grace.*

S*t. Catherine* of *Sienna,* conceived an ardent Defire to behold a Soul in Grace, and advantaged with all the Beauties thereof: Full of this Defire, fhe was no fooner departed from a Sermon, but fhe heard a Voice from Heaven, faying unto her, *Catherine, prefently thou fhalt fee the fruit of thy Defire.* And retiring her felf into her Oratory, fhe there befought God for the performance of his Promife, and fuddenly beheld a Perfon of incredible Majefty, all circled about with Light, and fhining with clear Splendor; at the fight of which, fhe was fo wrap't in Admiration, and Reverence, as fhe prefently proftrated her felf before its Feet, with intention to adore it, had it not with thefe words pro-hibited her: *Catherine forbear, for I am not God, as thou imagineft? And who then?* anfwered the Saint. *I am,* faid It, *the Soul of a certain Murtherer you prayed for, not long fince, in feeing me led to Execution; who being new cleanfed in the Fire of* Purgatory, *and going all purified to Heaven, after I fhall have left you fatisfied of your Defire by the Command-ment of Almighty God.*

An admirable Method to love, ferve, and honour the Bleffed Virgin Mary. Written in *Italian* by the R. F. *Alexis de Salo,* Ca-puchin : And Englifhed by R. F. *Permiffu Superiorum,* 1639. p. 179.

The Efficacy of the Rofary *to free a Soul from* Purgatory.

A T what time St. *Dominick* preached in the Kingdom of *Aragon,* a certain young Virgin of good account, called *Alexandria,* made Inftance unto him, as he came down from out of the Pulpit, (where he had omitted nothing that might make for the Commenda-tions of the *Rofary,*) to be admitted into the Sodality thereof; which fhe obtained, although for the reft, her Life was no ways according-ly, fhe being one who fpent much more time in adorning her Body,

has ever a ſpecial care of her devoted Servants, (though never ſo defective,) revealed the Fact unto St. *Dominick*, who, in order to her merciful Commands, went to the Pit, and called on *Alexandria* by her Name; when, behold! (a wondrous Accident,) the Angels, viſibly, in ſight of all the People, brought up the Head from the bottom of the Pit, which joined unto the Body. She beſought the Saint to hear her Confeſſion; which being done, ſhe declared three Things, worthy of particular Note, arrived unto her both before and after ſhe was dead. The firſt, That by vertue of her being of the Confraternity of the *Roſary*, ſhe had a perfect Act of Contrition at the Inſtant of her Death, without which, infallibly, ſhe had died Eternally. The ſecond, That as ſoon as ſhe was dead, the Devils putting her to great Afright, ſhe was marvellouſly ſecured and comforted by the glorious Queen of Heaven. The third, That for Penance, and ſatisfaction of the death of thoſe two Gentlemen, ſhe was condemned to *Purgatory* for Two hundred Years, and for Five hundred more, for her Vanity in Attire, the cauſe of that ſo lamentable effect; but that ſhe hoped, by the Merits of the ſame Confraternity, to be ſoon delivered from that Puniſhment. And having ſaid this, after ſhe had remained alive two whole days, for the Confirmation of the Miracle, and to augment the Devotions of the Sodality, ſhe left this Life again, whoſe Body was honourably Interred by the Sodaliſts there: When Fifteen days after, ſhe appeared again unto St. *Dominick* all in Glory, cloathed in reſplendent Beams of light, declaring unto him, after a world of Thanks for the ineſtimable Benefits ſhe had received of him, two Things of eſpecial Note concerning this Devotion of the *Roſary*. The one was, That ſhe was delegated to him from the Souls in *Purgatory*, with a Petition to be likewiſe inroll'd in the Sodality, to receive the benefit of it amongſt the reſt. The other, That the Angels much rejoiced at the Erection of this Sodality, and that God inſtiled himſelf the Father of it, the Bleſſed Virgin the Mother, &c. And having ſaid this, ſhe flew away to Heaven.

A Method to ſerve the Bleſſed Virgin Mary, *p.* 481, 482, 483, 484, 485.

Peter of *Clugny*, ſurnamed *the Venerable*, and eſteemed in his time as the Oracle of *France*, was a man who proceeded in theſe Affairs with much conſideration, not countenancing any thing either frivolous or light. Behold the Cauſe, wherefore I willingly make uſe of his Authority: He telleth, that in a Village of *Spain*, named *the Star*, there was a Man of Quality, called *Peter* of *Engelbert*, much eſteemed in the World for his excellent Parts, and abundant Riches.

Father *Cauſſin's Holy Court, p.*

Notwithstanding the Spirit of God had made him understand the Vanity of all humane Things, being now far stepped into years, he went into a Monastery of the Order of *Clugny*, there the more piously to pass the remnant of his days, as it is said, The best Incense cometh from old Trees. He often spake, among the Holy Friars, of a Vision which he saw, when he as yet was in the World, and which he acknowledged to be no small Motive to work his Conversion. This brute came to the Ears of venerable *Peter*, and who, for the affairs of his Order, was then gone into *Spain*. Behold the Cause why he, never admitting any Discourses to be entertained, if they were not well verified, took the pains to go into a little Monastery of *Nazare*, where *Engelbert* was, and to question him upon it in the presence of the Bishops of *Oleron*, and *Osma*, conjuring him, in the virtue of Holy Obedience, to tell him punctually the Truth touching the Vision he had seen, whil'st he led a secular Life. This Man being very grave, and very circumspect in all he said, spake the words which the Author of the History hath couched in his proper terms.

In the time that *Alphonsus* the younger, Heir of the great *Alphonsus*, warred in *Castile* against certain Factions disunited from his Obedience, he made an Edict, That every Family in his Kingdom should be bound to furnish him with a Soldier; which was the Cause, that for Obedience to the King's Commands, I sent into his Army one of my Houshold Servants, named *Sancius*. The Wars being ended, and the Troops discharged, he returned to my House, where having some time sojourned, he was seized by a Sickness, which, in few days, took him away into the other World. We performed the Obsequies usually observed towards the Dead, and four Months were already past, we heard nought at all of the state of his Soul, when, behold! upon a Winters Night, being in my Bed, throughly awake, I perceived a Man, who, stirring up the Ashes of my Hearth, opened the burning Coals, which made him the more easily to be seen. Although I found my self much terrified with the sight of this Ghost, God gave me Courage to ask him, *Who he was, and for what purpose he came thither to lay my Hearth abroad?* But he, in a very low voice answered, *Master, Fear nothing, I*

ample; Youth, and Temerity, all conspire against the Soul of a poor Soldier, who hath no Government. I committed many Outrages during the late War, robbing and pillaging, even to the Goods of the Church, for which I am at this present grievously tormented: But, good Master, if you loved me alive as one of yours, forget me not after death. I ask no part of your great Riches, but only your Prayers, and some Alms for my sake, which will much assist to mitigate my pain. My Mistrist oweth me about Eight Francks upon a Reckoning between her and me, let her not bestow it for my Body, which hath no need of it, but the comfort of my Soul, which expecteth it from your Charity.

I know not how I found my self emboldened by these Speeches, but I had more desire to entertain it, than fear of the Apparition. I demanded, Whether it could tell me News of one of my Countrymen, named *Peter Dejuca*, who died awhile since? To which he made Answer, *I need not trouble my self with it, for he was already in the number of the Blessed, since the great Alms he gave in the last Famine, had purchafed Heaven for him.* From thence I fell upon another Question, and was curious to know, What had hapned to a certain Judge, whom I very well knew, and who lately passed into the other Life? To which he replied, *Sir, Speak not of that miserable Man; for Hell possesseth him through the corruption of Justice which he, by damnable practice, exercised, having an Honour and Soul saleable to the prejudice of his Conscience.* My Curiosity carried me higher, to enquire what became of King *Alphonfus* the Great? At which time I heard another Voice that came from a Window behind me, saying, very distinctly, *It is not of Sancius you must demand that, because he, as yet, can say nothing of the state of that Prince; but I have more Experience thereof than he: I deceasing Five Years ago, and being present in an Accident which gave me some light of it.* I was much surprized, unexpectedly hearing this other Voice, and turning, saw, by the help of the Moons brightness, which reflected into my Chamber, a Man leaning on my Window, whom I entreated to tell me, Where then King *Alphonfus* was? Whereto he replied, *He will know, that passing out of this Life, he had been much tormented, and that the Prayers of good Religious Men much helped him; but he could not, at this present, say in what state he was.* Having spoken thus much, he turned towards *Sancius,* sitting near the Fire, and said, *Let us go, it is time we depart.* At which *Sancius* making no Answer, speedily rose up, and redoubled his Complaints, with a lamentable Voice, saying, *Sir, I entreat you, once again, remember me, and that my Mistrist perform the Request I made you.* The next day *Engelbert* understood from his Wife what the Spirit told him, and with all observation disposed himself speedily and charitably, to satisfie all was required.

*In the Universal Description of the Theater of Heaven and Earth,
by Joseph Rosaccio, Cosmographer and Doctor in Philosophy and
Physick, Printed at* Venice, 1620. *C.* 4. *Of the Extent of*
Hell, Purgatory, Limbus Patrum, *and* Abraham's Bosome.

THE Sphear of Hell, or to speak more properly, the Circumference of Hell, is the Lowest part of the Earth, and the Bigness
of it is about seven thousand, eight hundred and seventy five Miles.
The Breadth of it, that is to say the Diameter, is the third part of the
Circumference, or little less; and so are all Spherical Bodies. It is
distant from Us three thousand Miles, and seven hundred fifty eight,
and a quarter.

Above the Sphear of Hell is that of Purgatory, fifteen thousand,
seven hundred and fifty Miles in Circuit, and distant from Us two
thousand, five hundred and five Miles and a half.

Above the Sphear of Purgatory is that of *Limbus Patrum*, which is
twenty three thousand, six hundred and twenty five Miles, and distant
from Us one thousand, two hundred and fifty two Miles.

Above this is *Abraham*'s Bosome, much about the same length and
distance as the other.

Some object against this, that we have plac'd Hell lowermost, and
have made it less than the Earth, or any of the other Places, whereas
we ought to have made it bigger, in regard of the vast numbers of People
that have been crouding thither for these many thousand of years, and
never return, and will be daily crowding thither till the Worlds end.
To which we answer, That when the Center of the Universe shall be
remov'd out of the way, after the Day of Judgment, and the Earth,
with all that infinite heap of Mountains and Seas, shall be calcin'd to
nothing, there will be space enough; besides that, the Damned in
Chains and Fetters must not expect to have so much liberty as the
Saints in Heaven who are unconfin'd.

Miracles of the *British*, *English* and *Irish* SAINTS.

A Knight of Oxfordshire refusing to pay Tythes, One rais'd from the Dead convinces him of his Crime.

JOhn *Brompton*, Abbot of *Joreval*, and one of the *Decem Scriptores*, Col. 736. tells us, That St. *Austin*, (who was sent hither from *Rome*) once upon a time being to preach in the County of *Oxford*, at a Town which is called *Compton*, there came to him the Priest of the said Town, saying; *Father, may it please you to understand, that a Knight, the Lord of this Mannor, having been often admonished by me, will not pay the Tythes of those things which God has given him; and having threatned him with the Sentence of Excommunication, I have found him the more obstinate.* Which St. *Austin* hearing, when he had first sent for the Knight, said thus to him. *My Son, what is this which I hear of thee ? Why pay you not your Tythes to God and the Church ? Know you not that the Tythes are not yours, but God's?* To whom the Knight answered in wrath; *Who plowed or sowed the Land? Did not I? Know all men therefore, that to him belongs the tenth Sheaf, to whom belong the other nine.* To whom St. *Austin* replyed, *My Son, do not talk at this rate. For you may assure your self, that unless you pay your Tythes as other* Christian *People use to do, I will excommunicate you.* And turning to the Altar to say Mass, he said aloud before all the People, *I command that no Excommunicate Person be present at Mass.* At which Words a Dead Corpse which lay buried in the Entrance of the Church, rearing up it self, and going out into the Church-yard, stood there like a Statue all the while that St. *Austin* was saying Mass. Upon the sight of this, all the Faithful that were there present, being almost frighted out of their Wits, came to Blessed *Austin*, and told him what had happened ; To whom, saith he, *fear not. But let a Cross with the Holy Water go before Us, and let Us see what is the matter.* Whereupon *Austin* going along with the People, came with them to the Entrance of the Church yard, and when he saw the Dead Body, he said, *I command thee in the name of the Lord, that thou tell me who thou art.* To whom the Dead Man answered, *When on God's behalf you commanded that no Excommunicate Person should be present at Mass, the Angels of God, who are your constant Companions whereever you go, cast me out of the Place where I lay buried, saying, That the Friend of God,* Austin, *has commanded the stinking Flesh to be cast forth out of the Church of God.* For *in the time of the* Britains, *before the fury of the Pagan* Saxons *had wasted this Land,* I *was the Patron of this Parish. And though I was often admonished by the Priest of this Church,* I *never paid my Tythes ; and at length being excommunicated by him,* I *afterwards dyed, and was thrust down to* Hell. When they had heard this, both the Saint himself, and all the People that were with him, wept much. And *Austin* said, *Do you know the Place where the Priest was buried who excommunicated you?* Who answered, *he lies in this very Church-yard.* Go before Us, saith *Austin,* and shew Us the Place. The Dead Man went before, and came to a certain Place near the Church, where there appeared no sign at all of a Grave. And he said to *Austin,* and all the People that followed after him, *Lo this is the Place, dig here, and ye shall find the Bones of the Priest.* They digged therefore at St. *Austin's* bidding, and deep in the Earth they found a few Bones, which by the length of time were turned very dry. *Austin* asking whether these were the Bones of the Priest, the Dead Man answered, yes. Then *Austin* praying a good while, said, *That all may know that Life and Death are in the hands of God, to whom nothing is impossible ; In his name arise, for we have occasion for thee.* The words were no sooner out of his mouth, but all that were present saw the dispersed Dust come together, and the Bones to be compacted with Nerves, and the Man himself to rise up. The Priest thus standing before *Austin, Austin* saith to him, *Brother, Do you know that Man?* He answered, *Father,* I *do know him: and* I *wish* I *had not known him.* Quoth *Austin, You excommunicated him.* Quoth the Dead Priest, *I did so, and I had reason. For he was always a withholder of Tythes from the Church, and a Flagitious Man to his last day.* *Austin* replied, *Brother, You know that God is merciful, and therefore you ought likewise to have mercy upon the Creature and Image of God, who was also redeemed with his Blood, and has so long endured the pains of* Hell. Then he put a Whip into his hand, and the Other begging lamentably for Absolution upon his knees, the Dead Priest released the Sins of the Dead Patron. Whom being now absolved, *Austin* commanded to return to his Grave, and wait for the Last Day. And as soon as he was returned to his Grave, he immediately fell all into Ashes. Then saith *Austin* to the Priest, *How long have you lain here?* He made answer, *an hundred and fifty years and upwards.* Quoth *Austin, And how have you fared all this while? very well,* quoth the Priest, *and among the Delights of Eternal Life.* Then said *Austin, Would you be willing to have me pray to the Lord that you may return to live amongst us, and to help us by preaching to bring back Souls to their Creator, which are now beguiled by the Devil?* God forbid, *Father,* saith the Priest, *that I should be disturbed from my Rest ; and that you should cause me to return again to the Toilsome Life of this World* : Then said *Austin* to the Priest, *My Dear Friend, go and rest in peace, and withal, pray for me, and all the Holy Church of God.* Who entring into his Grave, was presently turned into Ashes. Then *Austin* called the Knight to him, and said, *How now Son, will you yet pay your Tythes to God?* But the Knight trembling, fell down at his feet, weeping and confessing his guilt, and begging pardon; and having left all that he had in the World, and shaved his Crown, he followed St. *Austin* all the days of his life, and closed his last day in all Holiness, and entred into the joy of Eternal Happiness.

The Wonderful Consecration of Westminster-*Abby by St.* Peter *himself.*

Eldred In
vit. Ed.
Confess.
Cressey's
Ch. Hist.
p. 308.

ELdred, Abbot of Rievall, gives this following Account; That in the time when King *Ethelred*, by the Preaching of St. *Austin*, embraced the Christian Faith: his Nephew *Sigebert*, who governed *East Angles* (rather *East Saxon*,) by the same holy Bishop's Ministry received the Faith. This Prince built one Church within the Walls of *London*, the principal City of the Kingdom; where he honourably placed *Militus* Bishop of the same City without the Walls: Likewise towards the West he founded a Famous Monastery to the honour of St. *Peter*, and endowed it with many Possessions. Now on the Night before the Day design'd for the Dedication of this Church, the blessed Apostle St. *Peter* appear'd to a certain Fisher-man in the habit of a Stranger, on the other side of the River of *Thames*, which flowed by this Monastery, demanded to be waft over, which was done: Being out of the Boat, he entered into the Church in the sight of the Fisher-men; and presently a heavenly Light shone so clear, that it turned the Night into Day. There was with the Apostle a multitude of Heavenly Citizens, coming out, and going into the Church: A Divine Melody sounded, and an Odour of an unexpressible fragrancy was shed abroad. As soon as all things pertaining to the Dedication of the Church was performed, the glorious Fisher of Men returned to the poor Fisher-man, who was so affrighted with his Divine Splendour, that he almost lost his Senses: But St. *Peter* kindly comforted him, brought him to himself; then both of them entered into the Boat: St. *Peter* asked him if he had any Provision; Who answered, that partly being stupified with seeing so great a Light, and partly detained by his return, he had taken nothing; being withal assured of a good Reward from him: hereto the Apostle replyed, Let down thy Net: The Fisher-man obeyed, and immediately the Net was filled with a multitude of Fishes: They were all of the same kind, except one Salmon, of a wonderful largeness. Having then drawn them to fhoar, St. *Peter* faid ; *Carry from me this great Fifh to* Militus *the Bifhop, and all the reft take for thy hire. And moreover be affured, That both Thou, all thy life-time, and thy Children after thee, for many years, fhall be plentifully furnifhed with thofe kind of Fifhes ; only be careful that you fifh not on the Lord's Day. I who fpeak now with thee,* am Peter. *And I my felf have Dedicated this Church, built to my Fellow-Citizens, and to my Honour, fo preventing by my own Authority the Epifcopal Benediction. Acquaint the Bifhop therefore with the things that thou haft feen and heard, and the Signs yet marked in the Wall will confirm thy Speeches. Let him therefore furceafe from his Defign of Confecrating the Church, and only fupply what I have omitted ; The Celebration of the Myftery of Our Lord's Body and Blood, and the Inftruction of the People ; Let him likewife give notice to all, That I my felf will oftentimes vifit this Place, and be prefent at the Prayers of the Faithful, and will open the Gates of Heaven to all that live Soberly, Juftly and Pioufly in this World.* And as foon as he had faid this, he prefently vanifhed from his fight.

The next Morning, as the Bifhop *Militus* was going in proceffion to the Church with an intention to Dedicate it, the Fifher-man met him with the Fifh, and related to him whatfoever St. *Peter* had injoin'd him ; at which the Bifhop was aftonifhed, and having unlocked the Church-door, he faw the Pavement marked with Letters and Infcriptions both in Greek and Latin, and the Walls anointed in twelve feveral places with holy Oyl. He faw likewife the remainder of twelve Torches, fticking on as many Croffes, and the Church every-where yet moift with Afperfions. All which being obferved by the Bifhop, and People prefent, they rendered praife and thanks to Almighty God.

The fame Author relates, That the Children of this Fifher-man, having received a command from their Father, of paying the Tythes of all their Gain by fifhing, and offer'd them to St. *Peter* and the Priefts attending Divine Service in this Church : But one amongft them having prefumed to defraud the Church of this, prefently was deprived of the wonted benefit of his Trade ; till having confeft his Fault, and reftored what he had referved, he promifed amendment for the future.

William of *Malmsbury* adds to this Story ; That the Fifher-man, who was very fimple, and as yet not a Chriftian, difcovered to the Bifhop very exactly the Shapes and Lineaments of St. *Peter*, well known to the Bifhop by his Picture publickly extant at *Rome*.   Malmf. *de* Geft. Pontific. L. 2.

In the Year 635. fays Father *Creffy*, S. *Birinus*, being advifed by Pope *Honorius* to repair into *Britany* for the Converfion of the *Weft-Saxons*, does affert this *Apoftolick Miffion* of S. *Birinus*, our Lord, to have been approved by a Divine Miracle ; and for the truth of his Affertion, quotes *Baronius*, who cites for it, as he fays, *William* of *Malmsbury*, *Huntingdon*, *Florentius*, *Mathew* of *Weftminfter*, &c.   P. 350.

I have thought expedient, faith he, *to defcribe here out of the Acts of St.* Birinus *a wonderful Miracle befeeming an Apoftolick Man, which is omitted by St.* Beda. *It was thus : The Holy Man being arrived to the Shore of the Britifh Sea, and ready to take Ship, celebrated the Divine Myfteries, offering to God the Sacrifice of the Saving Hoft as a* Viaticum *for himfelf and Followers. After which, the Seafon being proper, he was haftily urged to enter the Ship: and the Wind ferving them, they failed fpeedily, when on the fudden Birinus called to mind that he had loft a thing infinitely precious to him, which by the urging haft of the Seamen, having his mind other ways bufied, he had left behind him at Land. For Pope* Honorius *had beftowed on him a* Pall, *or Corporal, upon which he confecrated the Body of our Lord, and afterward ufed to wear it in a Particle of the faid Sacred Body, which he hung about his Neck, and always carried with him: but when he celebrated Mafs, he was wont to lay it by him upon the Altar. Armed therefore with Faith, he by Divine Infpiration went down from the Ship into the Sea, and walk'd fecurely upon it to the Shore. Where finding what he had left behind, he took it, and in like manner returned to the Ship, which he found ftanding ftill immoveable, whereas a little before he had left it failing extreme fwiftly. When he was entred into the Ship, not one drop of water appeared on his Cloaths; which the Mariners feeing, kneel'd before him, and worfhipped him as a God: and many of them by his Preaching were converted to the Faith of Chrift.*

How St. Edmund's *Head was miraculoufly found, and interred with his Body.*

St. *Edmund,* King of the *Eaft-Angles,* having had his Army under the Command of the valiant Count *Walketule* routed by the *Danes,* in the time of their Invafion of this Ifland, that Pious King was likewife, after fome farther Oppofition, taken by them; and being tied to a Tree by order of their General, was firft moft cruelly whipped, and then thofe Barbarians did, as it were in fport, fo pierce with their Darts his whole Body in all places, that in a fhort time there was not left place for a new Wound; yet he willingly fuftaining all thefe Torments for the *Faith* of *Chrift,* and Defence of his Countrey, they cut off his Head.

But the Rage and Malicious Fury of thofe *Pagans* not ceafing after they had thus flain King *Edmund;* but cafting out his Body defpightfully, they kept the Head to revenge themfelves yet further on the Tongue which had fo conftantly founded forth the Name of *Chrift :* and after they had ufed all manner of Contemptuous Scorns upon it, they caft it into a fecret place in a thicket of a Wood adjoining, left the *Chriftians* fhould venerate it, and decently bury it with the Body.

There it remained a whole years fpace: after which the *Pagans* retiring out of the Countrey, the firft care of the *Chriftians* was to honour their Holy King and Martyr. Affembling themfelves therefore together out of their lurking Places, they reverently took his Body out of the unclean Place where it had been caft, and then with all diligence fought for the Head. And whilft every one of them with equal Affection fearched each corner of the Wood, there hapned a Wonder not heard of in any Age before. For whilft they difpers'd themfelves in all parts, and each one demanded of his Companions, where it was that the *Danes* had caft the Head, the fame *Head* anfwered them aloud in their own Tongue, *Here, here, here:* neither did it ceafe to cry out in the fame Words till it had brought them to the Place. And to add to the Wonder, there they found a mighty and fierce Wolf, which with its Fore-feet held the Head, as if appointed to watch and defend it from other Beafts. When they were come, the Wolf quietly refigned it to them: fo with joyful Hymns to God they carried and joyn'd it to the Body, the Wolf in the mean time following it to the Place where they buried it; after which, the Beaft returned into the Wood: In all which time, neither did the Wolf hurt any one, neither did any one fhew the leaft Intention to hurt the Wolf. *F. Creffy's* Church Hiftory, P. 734, 735, 736.

A Monk Divinely punifhed for his neglect to venerate the Holy Crofs.

A Monk of *Glaftenbury* named *Ailfi*, refufing to bow, as others did, to a Crucifix; at laft, either out of Compunction, or by Command of his Superior, he bowed himfelf: but a Voice proceeding from the Image, faid thefe words diftinctly; *Now too late* Ailfi, *now too late* Ailfi: Which Voice fo affrighted him, that falling down, he prefently expired.

F. Creffy's Church Hiftory, p. 876.

St. Dunftan's *Miracles.*

ONce upon a time, a mighty Beam, from the top of the Church, threatning the Deftruction of many by its fall, St. *Dunftan* with his Right hand making the fign of the Crofs, lift it up again.

Sarisbury Breviary, Leffon. 3.

Further, As this Saint was praying one Night, the Devil affails him in the fhape of a Bear, and endeavoured with his Teeth to fnatch the Staff out of his Hands, upon which the Man of God leaned; he unaffrighted lifts up his Staff, and followed the horrid Monfter, beating him, and finging thefe words: *Let God arife, and let his Enemies be fcattered.* And the Ugly Phantafm vanifhed.

A Miracle to affert the Real Prefence.

WHen St *Odo* was celebrating the Mafs in the prefence of certain of the Clergy of *Canterbury* (who maintained that the Bread and Wine, after Confecration, do remain in their former fubftance, and are not *Chrift's* true Body and Blood, but a Figure of it:) When he was come to Confraction, prefently the Fragments of the Body of *Chrift* which he

F. Creffy's Church Hiftory, p. 842.

held in his hands, began to pour forth blood into the Chalice. Whereupon he shed tears of joy; and beckning to them that wavered in their Faith, to come near and see the wonderful Work of God; as soon as they beheld it, they cryed out, O holy Prelate, to whom the Son of God has been pleased to reveal himself visibly in the Flesh, pray for us, that the Blood we see here present to our Eyes, may again be changed, but for our Unbelief the Divine Vengeance fall upon us; he prayed accordingly; after which, looking into the Chalice, he saw the Species of Bread and Wine, where he had left Blood.

How our Saviour let St. Wittekundus *know the Worthy and Unworthy Receivers.*

Bolland.
*in vita e-
jus, ad*
Jan. 7.
p. 38 4.
St. *Wittekundus* in the Administration of the *Eucharist*, saw a Child enter into every ones Mouth, playing and smiling when some received him, and with an abhorring Countenance when he went into the Mouths of others; *Christ* thus shewing this Saint in his Countenance, who were Worthy, and who Unworthy Receivers.

St. Wereburga's *Wild-Goose Miracle.*

Malmsbur.
de Pontif.
L. 4.
Ap. Caprav.
S. Wereburga.
THE Memory of *Wulfere*, King of the *Mercians*, received a great lustre from the wonderful Sanctity of his Daughter St. *Wereburga*, Who after her Father's Death undertook a Religious Profession, and by her Brother was persuaded to accept the Government of three Monasteries of Religious Virgins, *Frickingham*, since called *Trent*, in *Staffordshire*, *Wedum* and *Hamburgh* in *Northamtonshire*. In this Station she not only found due Obedience from her Devout Daughters, but even Irrational and Wild Creatures became subject to her Command, as if by her Sanctity she had recovered that Empire which Man enjoy'd in his Primitive Innocence. This will be made appear by her banishing from her Territory great flocks of Wild Geese for their Importunity and wastful Devouring her Corn and other Fruits. The manner of it was as followeth.

There was near the Walls of the Town a Farm belonging to the Monastery, the Corn whereof was much wasted by Flocks of wild Geese, which the Steward of the place endeavoured, but in vain, to

that a certain Servant, privately, ftole one of the fame Birds, which he hid, with intention to eat it. The next morning, early, the Holy Virgin went to the Houfe, where, after fhe had, in a Chiding manner, reprehended the Birds for ufurping that which belonged not to them, fhe commanded them to flie away, and not return. Immediately the whole Army of them took wing ; but being fenfible of the injury done them, they flew not away, but hovering over the Holy Virgins head, with wonderful noife, made complaint of their lofs. She hearing their importunate Clamours, underftood, by Infpiration, the caufe thereof ; and, after fearch made, the Offender confeffed his Theft ; whereupon fhe commanded the Bird to be reftored to her Companions. After which they all, with one confent, flew away, fo as that not any Bird of that kind was afterwards feen in that Territory. And *William* of *Malmsbury* affirms, That the ftolen Bird was kill'd, and again reftored to life by the Saint. *F. Creffi's Church-Hiftory*, p. 427.

Of St. Juftinian's *being beheaded, and of his croffing the Seas on foot afterwards, with his Head in his hand.*

St. *Juftinian* was born of a Noble Family in *Leffer Britany*, where, after having fpent his Youth in Study and Learning, he received the Order of Priefthood. Then he travelled, and at length came to an Ifland, then called *Lemeicy*, now *Ramfy*. Afterwards he became St. *David's* Confeffor, and a mighty Promoter of Chriftianity. This fet the Devil to work againft him ; and by that Enemy of Mankind's Inftigation, three of this Holy Mans-Servants, who had been reprov'd by him for their Idlenefs, and mifpending their time, rufht upon him, threw him to the ground, and moft cruelly cut off his Head. But in the place where the facred Head fell to the ground, a Fountain of pure Water prefently flow'd, by drinking of which, in following times, many were, miraculoufly, reftored to health.

But Miracles, greater than thefe, immediately fucceeded his death: For the Body of the bleffed Martyr prefently rofe, and taking the Head between the two Arms, went down to the Sea fhore, and walking thence on the Sea, paffed over to the Port called by his Name ; and being arriv'd in the place where a Church is new built to his memory, it fell down, and was there buried by St. *David*, with fpiritual Hymns and Canticles : In which Church our Lord vouchfafes frequently to atteft the Sanctity of his Servant by many Miracles. F. Creffi's *Church-Hiftory*, p. 234.

Ap. Capgrav. In Juftiniano,

How S. Ositha *walk'd, when dead, with her Head in her hands, and knock'd at a Church-door.*

Baron. ad
A. D. 653.

St. *Ofitha* was Daughter of a *Mercian* Prince, named *Frithwald*, and of *Wilterburga*, Daughter of *Pende*, King of the *Mercians.* She was bred up in great Piety, and, through her Parents Authority, became Wife to *Sighere*, Companion of S. *Seb.* in the Kingdom of the *Eaſt Angles.* But preferring the Love of a heavenly Bridegroom, before the Embraces of a King, her Husband complied with her Devotion ; and, moreover, not only permitted her to confecrate her felf to our Lord, but beſtowed on her a Village, fituated near the Sea, called *Chic*, where building a Monaftery, ſhe enclofed her felf. And after ſhe had fpent fome time in the ſervice of God, it hapned that a Troop of *Daniſh* Pirats landed there; who, going out of their Ships, waſted and burnt the Countrey thereabout, ufing all manner of Cruelty againſt the Chriftian Inhabitants. Then he who was the Captain of that impious Band, having learnt the Condition and Religious Life of the bleſſed Virgin St. *Ofitha*, began, by Entreaties, and Prefents, to tempt her to Idolatry ; adding withal, Threats of Scourging, and other Torments, if ſhe refufed to adore the gods which he worſhipped: But the Holy Virgin defpifing his Flatteries, and not fearing his Threats, made fmall account of the Torments attending her. Whereupon the faid Captain, enraged at her Conftancy, and fcorn of his Idols, pronounced Sentence of Death againſt her, commmanding her to lay down her Head to be cut off. And in the fame place where the Holy Virgin fuffered Martyrdom, a clear Fountain broke forth, which cured feveral kinds of Difeafes. As foon as her Head was off, the Body prefently rofe up, and taking up the Head in the hands, by the conduct of Angels, walked firmly the ftraight way to the Church of the Apoſtles St. *Peter*, and St. *Paul*, about a quarter of a Mile diftant from the place of her fuffering: And when it was come there, it knocked at the Door with the bloody hands, as defiring it might be opened, and thereon left marks of Blood. Having done this, it fell there down to the ground ; now her Parents having heard of her death, earneftly defired, as fome recompence for their lofs, to enjoy the comfort of burying with them her headlefs Body : which being brought to them, they. Interred it in a Coffin of Lead in the Church of *Aylesbury*, where ma-; ny Miracles were wrought by her Interceſſion. At length, her facred Reliques, by a Divine Vifion, were tranflated thence, back again to the Church of *Chic*, which *Maurice*, Biſhop of *London*, repofed in a precious Coffer ; at which time the Biſhop of *Rocheſter*, then prefent, was cured of a grievous Infirmity. F. *Creſſy's Church-Hiſtory*, p. 424.

Harcus in
Martyro-
log. 7.
Octob.

Capgrav.
in S. Oſi-
tha.

The Hiftory of St. Claire, *a Martyr to Chaftity.*

St. *Claire,* by Birth an *Englifh-man,* of a very Noble Defcent, and Il- luftrious for his outward Comelinefs, inward natural Endowments, fingular Piety, rare Chaftity. Being at years of maturity, his Parents would have matcht him to a Noble and Beautiful Virgin: But, to pre- ferve his Virginal Purity, on his very Marriage day he ftole away into *France,* where he efpous'd an Hermit's life, and fpent his days in ftrict Exercifes of Piety. But the Enemy of Man's falvation could not long fupport the brightnefs of Divine Graces fhining in this Saint; to obfcure which, he inflamed, with Luft, the Mind of a certain Noble-woman dwelling near, who immediately attempted to expugn the Chaftity of the Servant of God: But St. *Claire* refolutely refifted the fhamelefs Lady; notwithftanding which refiftance, when her Sollicitations more increafed, he was forced, for his own quietnefs and liberty, to forfake his Monaftery.

The lafcivious Woman, defperately enraged with his departure, fent two Murderers in fearch of him, who, at laft, found him in a poor Cottage, where he had fixed his Habitation with one onely Compa- nion, named *Cyrinus.* There they firft fet upon him with many oppro- brious Speeches, and, at laft, drawing out their Swords, they moft cruelly cut off his Head, whil'ft he, devoutly kneeling, offered his Sa- crifice of Chaftity to our Lord, the Lover of pure Minds, and Patron of Innocence.

This glorious Champion of Chaftity being thus victorious by Pa- tience, prefently after arofe, and with his hands taking up his Head, by the affiftance of Angels, carried it to a Fountain, not far diftant, into which he caft it; and then carried the fame back to the Oratory of his Cell; and going on a little further, towards a Village feated near the River *Epta,* which fince took a new Name from this glorious Mar- tyr, he there confummated his Courfe, and tranfmitted his bleffed Soul to Heaven. As for his Companion *Cyrinus,* he being firft dangeroufly wounded, was, by the Prayers of St. *Clarus,* wonderfully reftored to health. The diftinct place where this holy Martyr fuffered, is faid to be in the Territory near *Rouen* in *Normandy,* near the River *Seyne.*

Martyro- log. Gall. 4. *Novemb.*

Ap Cap- grav. in S. Claro.

S. Decumanus *does himfelf wafh his own Head, after it was cut off.*

St. *Decumanus,* born of Noble Parents in the South-weftern parts of *Wales,* forfaking his Countrey, the more freely to give himfelf to Mortification, and Devotion, paffed the River *Severne* upon a Hurdle of Rods, and retired himfelf into a mountainous vaft Solitude covered

A. D. 706. *Martyr. Angl.* 27. *Auguft. Capgrav.*

*Ap. Cap-
grav.*

But it fo hapned, that when his Head was cut from his Body, the Trunk raifing it felf up, took the Head, which it carrieds from the place where he was flain, to a Spring not far off, which flowed with a moft chryftal Water, in which, with the Hands, it wafhed the Blood away; which Spring, in memory of the Saint, is, to this day, called St. *Decumanfis's* Spring, near to which place the Body, together with the Head, was Honourably buried by the neighbouring Inhabitants. F. *Creffi's Church-Hiftory,* p. 526.

S. Ruadanus, *and* S. Finnian, *Counter-Miracle one another.*

*Colganus
vita Fin-
niani* 23
Febr. p.
595.

St. *Ruadanus* obtained this fpecial favour of God, that from a certain Tree in his Cell (*Tilia* it's call'd) from the hour of Sun-fetting till Nine a Clock the next Day, dropt a Liquor of a peculiar tafte, pleafing to every Palate; which then fill'd a Veffel, which fufficed for a Dinner for him and all his Brotherhood: and from Nine a Clock to Sun-fetting it dropt half a Veffel full, with which Strangers were entertained. Upon the fame of this Miracle many of the Saints came to St. *Finnian,* defiring him to go along with them to that place, and perfuade *Ruadanus* to live a Life common with others. St. *Finnian* went with them, and when they came to the Tree that gave the admirable Liquor, he fign'd it with the fign of the Crofs, and after Nine a Clock the Liquor ceas'd to flow. St. *Ruadanus* hearing that his Mafter S. *Finnian,* and feveral others were come to him, he called his Servant, and bid him prepare a Dinner for his Guefts; who going to the Tree, he found the Veffel that ftood under it wholly empty, and told his Mafter how it was; who bid him carry his Veffel to the Fountain, and fill it to the top with Water, which when he had done, prefently the Water was changed into the tafte of that Liquor which dropt from the Tree. Moreover, he found a Fifh of great bignefs in the Fountain, and carried all to the Man of God; who commanded him to fet thefe Gifts before St. *Finnian.* He feeing what was done, Croffed the Liquor, and it was changed again into common Water, and faid, *Why is this Liquor of a falfe Name given unto me?* The Difciples of St. *Finnian* feeing all this, defired their Mafter to go to the Fountain, and Crofs it, as he had done the Tree: But St. *Finnian* anfwered them, *My Brethren, do not grieve this holy Man, for if he go before us to the next Bog, he will be able to do the fame that he did in the Tree, and the Water, namely, make fuch Liquor flow thence.* Wherefore St. *Finnian,* and the reft, all entreated St. *Ruadanus,* that he would live as others did; which he yielded to, and he held the common courfe of living.

St. Auguftin's *Miracle.*

St. *Auguftin* difputing with the *Britifh* Bifhops about the Obfervation of *Eafter*, and arguing, That they did not keep it in its due time: When the *Britains*, after a long Difputation, would not be moved to give their Affent, but would follow their own Traditions, St. *Auguftin* brought the Difpute to this Conclufion, faying, *Let us befeech our Lord, who makes Brethren of one mind in the Houfe of his Father, that he would vouchfafe, by Celeftial Signs, to make known unto us, which of the Traditions is to be followed, and which is the right Path leading to his Kingdom. Let fome Perfon be here produced among us; and he by whofe Cares he fhall be cured, let that Man's Faith and Practice be believed acceptable to God, and to be followed by Men.* This Propofition being accepted, with much ado, a blind Man was brought before them, and was firft offered to the *Britifh* Bifhops, but by their Endeavors and Miniftry found no Cure and Help. At length *Auftin*, compelled thereto by juft Neceffity, kneeled down, and prayed to God to reftore the blind Man his fight; whereupon, immediately, the blind Man (upon his Prayer) received fight, and *Auftin* was proclaimed by all a true Preacher of Celeftial Light.

Father Creffy's Church-Hiftory. l.13. c.18.

B. l.2. c.2.

St. Keyna *turns Serpents into Stones.*

THE Holy *Britifh* Virgin St. *Keyna* was Illuftrious for her Birth, being the Daughter of *Braganus*, Prince of that Province of *Wales*, which, from him, was called *Brecknockfhire*; but more Illuftrious for her Zeal to preferve her Chaftity, for which fhe was call'd, in the *Britifh* Tongue *Keynvayre*, that is, *Keyna* the Virgin. When fhe came to ripe years, many Noble Perfons fought her in Marriage, but fhe utterly forfook that ftate, having confecrated her Virginity to our Lord by a perpetual Vow. At length fhe determined to forfake her Countrey, and find out fome defart place where fhe might attend to Contemplation; wherefore directing her Journey beyond *Severn*, and coming to certain woody places, fhe requefted the Prince of that Countrey, that fhe might be permitted to ferve God in that Solitude. The Prince was willing to grant her Requeft, only he told her, *The place did fo fwarm with Serpents, that neither Man nor Beafts could inhabit in it.* To which fhe replied, *That her Truft was fixed in the Name and Affiftance of Almighty God, and therefore fhe doubted not to drive all that poyfonous brood out of that Region.* Hereupon the place was readily granted to the Holy Virgin, who proftrating her felf to God in fervent Prayer, obtain'd of him to change all the Serpents and Vipers there into Stones; fo as to this day the Stones, in that Region, refemble the windings of Serpents through all the Fields and Villages, as if they had been fo fram'd by the hand of the Engraver.

The ftate of Church Affairs in this Ifland under Britifh Kings.

F

The

The Hiſtory of St. David, *and his Miracles.*

The ſtate
of Church
Affairs in
this Iſland
under the
Britiſh
Kings. P.
115. Lon-
don. Prin-
ted by N.
Thompſ.
1687,

THE King of the Region, call'd *Ceretica,* travelling to *Dunetia,* met, by the way, a Religious Virgin, call'd *Nonnita,* of great Beauty ; which he luſting after, by Violence deflowr'd ; She, hereby, conceiv'd a Son, but neither before nor after had ever knowledge of any Man. The King thus Father of St. *David,* is call'd *Xanthus* ; and his Mother, by ſome, nam'd *Melaria* ; others, *Nonnita.* His Eminency was predicted by St. *Patrick* long before: For that Saint being in the Valley of *Roſina,* in the Province of *Dimeta* (*North-Weſt Wales*) meditating on his Miſſion into *Ireland,* had a Revelation by an Angel, *That after Thirty Years a Child ſhould be born in that Province, which ſhould give a great Luſtre to that Countrey.* And his Nativity was uſher'd in by another Miracle : For when *Gildas Albanius* was, from the Pulpit, teaching a great Congregation, on the ſudden he became dumb, and unable to ſpeak, but afterwards broke forth into theſe words: *A Holy Woman,* call'd *Nonnita, now preſent in this Church, is great with Child, and ſhall ſhortly be brought to Bed of a Son, full repleniſht with Grace. It was in regard to him that I was hindred from ſpeaking, by a Divine Power reſtraining my Tongue. This Child ſhall be of ſo eminent Sanctity, that none in theſe our Parts are comparable to him ; I will ſurrender this Region to him, who will from his Infancy, by degrees, increaſe in Grace and Sanctity: An Angel, God's Meſſenger, hath revealed this unto me.* This Holy Child, not long after born, being baptiz'd, and growing up in Grace, became the firſt Biſhop of *Menevia,* to which place he tranſlated the Biſhoprick of *Caerleon,* and which, from him, was called St. *Davids.*

The ſtate
of Church
Affairs
under the
Britiſh
Kings, p.
238.

Now in the Year of Grace 519, a *Britiſh* Synod being aſſembled, on the occaſion of the deteſtable Hereſie of the *Pelagians, Paulin,* a Biſhop with whom St. *David* in his Youth had been educated, earneſtly perſuaded the Fathers to ſend for St. *David* in the Name of the Synod, who was lately conſecrated Biſhop by the Patriarch, to afford his aſſiſtance to God's Church now in great danger; but could not prevail with him to forſake his Contemplations, until, at laſt, two Holy Men, *Daniel,* and *Dubritius,* by their Authority brought him to the Synod ; And then all the Fathers there aſſembled, enjoin'd St. *David* to preach. He commanded a Child, which had lately been reſtor'd to Life by him, to ſpread a Napkin under his Feet, and ſtanding upon it, he began to expound the Goſpel and the Law to the Auditory. All the while he continued, a ſnow white Dove deſcending from Heaven, ſate upon his ſhoulder, and the Earth, on which he ſtood, rais'd it ſelf under him, till it became a Hill, from whence his Voice, like a Trumpet, was clearly heard and underſtood by all both far and near: On the top of which

Hill

Hill a Church was afterwards built, which remains to this day. When the Sermon was finifht, fo powerfully did Divine Grace co-operate, that the Herefie foon vanifh'd , and was extinguifh'd ; and the Holy Bifhop St. *David* , by the general Election and Approbation both of Clergy and People, was exalted to be Archbifhop of all *Cambria.* Now concerning the fame *Paulin* or *Paulins* that fent for *David* to the Synod, we find that St. *David*, as foon as he was promoted to the Prieft-   *Ib. p.* 141. hood, went to *Paulins*, a Difciple of St. *German* ; and that in a certain Ifland he led a Holy Life acceptable to God, and that St. *David* liv'd with him many years, and follow'd his Inftructions. *Paulinus*, at laft, by extreme pains in his Eyes, loft the ufe of them ; whereupon calling his Difciples together, he defired that one after another they would look upon his Eyes, and fay a Prayer or Benediction on them : But receiving no Benefit thereby, *David* faid to him, *Father, Command me not to look you in the Face ; for Ten Years are paft fince I ftudied the Scriptures with you, and in all that time I never had the boldnefs to look you in the Face.* Paulins, admiring his Humility, faid, *Since it is fo, it will fuffice, if by touching mine Eyes , thou pronounce a Benediction on them.* Prefently therefore, as foon as he had toucht them, Sight was reftored to them. When St. *David* came to dye, our Lord Jefus vouchfafed him his Prefence, as he had promis'd by his Angel, to the infinite Confolation of the Holy Father : And St. *Kentigern* faw a multitude of Angels conducting him into the Joy of our Lord ; and our Lord   *Ib. p.* 146 himfelf, at the Entrance of Paradife, crowning him with Glory and Honour.

St. Winwaloe's *Sifters Eye being pluckt out by a Goofe , he opens the Goofe, reftores his Sifter to her Eye, and the Goofe to her Life.*

St. *Winwaloe's* Sifters Eye being pluckt out as fhe was playing by a   *Act. San-* Goofe, he was taught by an Angel a fign whereby to know that   *ctor.Mart.* Goofe from the reft about the Houfe, and having cut it open, found the   3. *p.* 25. Eye in its Entrails, preferved by the power of God uhhurt, and fhining like a Gem ; which he took, and put it in again in its proper place, and recovered his Sifter : And was fo kind alfo to the Goofe , as to fend it away alive , after it had been cut up, to the reft of the Flock.

An Obedient Fox puniſht for ſtealing a Saint's Hen.

Bull. *Act.*
Sanct. in
vit. Ge-
nulph. *ad*
Jan. 17.

A Fox having ſtol one of S. *Genulph's* Hens, he chid the Fox, and commanded him to lay it down juſt in the place whence he took it; all which the Fox performed; but could not ſo eſcape, but was miraculouſly puniſht for his Theft; for as he was running away by the Door of the Church, he fell down dead.

The Miracle of the Red Sea *repeated.*

The State
of Church
Affairs in
this Iſland
under Bri-
tiſh *Kings,*
p. 89.

WHile St. *Patrick* labour'd with great ſucceſs in the Goſpel, *Britain* was illuſtrated with the Memory of another great Saint *Winwaloe*, the Son of a Noble Perſon called *Fracon*, Couſin-german of a *Britiſh* Prince nam'd *Coton.* This S. *Winwaloe* was from his Childhood inflam'd with an earneſt deſire to live to God only; and having got leave of his Parents to be commended to the care of a certain Religious Man, he made great Progreſſes in Vertue and Holineſs; and in proceſs of time undertook a Monaſtical Profeſſion. Many Miracles God wrought by him, in performance whereof, having a firm Faith, he made uſe only of the Sign of the Croſs, and Oyl which had been bleſſed: Amongſt which Miracles the moſt ſtupendious was, his raiſing a Young Man to Life.

At this time the Glory of the moſt Holy Prelate St. *Patrick* was famous in God's Church, who like a Bright Star illuſtrated all *Ireland*; and the report of his admirable Vertues kindled in St. *Winwaloe* ſo great an Affection towards him, that he endeavoured to paſs over to him; and be ſubject to his Direction in Piety. Behold, while the Holy Man's thoughts were buſied about this Deſign, St. *Patrick* in a Viſion preſented himſelf to him with an Angelical Brightneſs, and a golden Diadem on his head, telling him he was the ſame *Patrick*, whom he ſo earneſtly deſired to viſit: But to prevent a dangerous Journey by Sea and Land, our Lord hath ſent me to thee to fulfil thy deſire, ſo as thou mayſt enjoy both my ſight and Converſation: he further told St. *Winwaloe*, that he ſhould be a Guide and Director of many in Spirituals.

The Baron of Honſden's *Viſion.*

IN the Year 1596. the Baron of *Honſden*, who had been formerly of *Elizabeth*, the Queen of *England*'s Council, falling dangerouſly ill, ſaw entring into his Chamber ſix of the Principal Officers of this Kingdom, who dyed a little before, and had as well as he been cruel Perſecutors of the Catholick Religion. They appeared almoſt all ſurrounded with flames; and in that diſmal eſtate, drawing near his Bed, they bid him acquaint *William Cecil*, one of the Accomplices of their Impieties and their Violences, that in a little time he ſhould deſcend into Hell, there with them to fuffer the Punifhment that was due to fo many Crimes. After they were vanifh'd, the Sick Man related the Vifion he had had, and affirmed with Oaths that it was no *Reverie*, but a certain Truth. Neverthelefs he did not avail himfelf of it: For inftead of employing the remainder of his Life in doing fruits worthy of Penitence, he dy'd fome few days after in his Error, and in his Sin: *Cecil* quickly followed him, God having fnatcht him out of the World by a Death as fatal as it was fudden and unforefeen. *Le Pedag. Chrif. P. 265.*

The Miracles *by* Chrift's Blood.

Hᴀles in *Glouceferfhire*, where the Blood of Jefus Chrift, brought from *Jerufalem*, being kept (as was affirmed) for divers Ages, had drawn a great many great Offerings to it from remote Places: And it was faid to have this Property, That if a Man were in Mortal Sin, and not abfolved, he could not fee it; otherwife very well : Therefore every Man that came to behold this Miracle, confefs'd himfelf firft to a Prieft there, and then offering fomething to the Altar, was directed to a Chappel where the Relique was fhewed ; The Prieft who confefs'd him (in the mean while) retiring himfelf to the back part of the faid Chappel, and putting forth upon the Altar a Cabinet or Tabernacle of Chryftal, which being thick on the one fide, that nothing could be feen thorough it ; but on the other fide thin and tranfparent, they ufed diverfly: For if a rich and devout Man entred, they would fhew the thick fide, till he had paid for as many Maffes, and given as large Alms as they thought fit ; after which (to his great joy) they permitted him to fee the thin fide, and the Blood. Whether yet (as my Author, a Clerk of the Council to *Edward* the Sixth, and living in thefe times, affirms) was proved to be the Blood of a Duck, every week renewed by two Priefts, who kept the Secret between them.

L. Herbert's Hifory of Henry the Eighth, p. 494.

Miracles faid to be wrought by
St. *Thomas A Becket.*

St. Thomas A Becket *chufes the Bleffed Virgin for his Miftrefs, and She mends his Shirt for him.*

Sᴛ. *Thomas*, that Arch-ftickler againft the Prerogatives of the Crown and his King, to favour the Progreffes of Church-Privileges and the Interefts of the Pope, we are told, from his youth had vow'd his Chaftity to the Bleffed Virgin ; and being, on a time, among fome of his

Gemoni Chronicon. SS. Dei parve, p. 177

Companions (before he was Archbishop) he heard them boasting of
their Mistresses, and the special Presents they had received from them.
Thomas told them that they vapour'd foolishly, for he had a Mistress
that far excelled all theirs; who had bestowed such a Present on him,
that they never saw any thing like it. All   s he intended in a Spiritual
Sense ; but, they urging vehemently that h would shew them what he
talked of; he ran to the Church, and prayed the Blessed Virgin to pardon the Presumptuous Word he had spoken of her.   To whom she appeared in a Vision, and incouragingly told him , that he did well to cry
up the Excellency of his Mistress ; and she gave him a very fine and a
very little Box , which his Companions snatcht out of his hand, and
opening, saw something of a Purple Colour, and taking it out, behold
a wonderful fine *Casula*,(a Garment which the Priests wear.) This Story
came to the ears of the Archbishop of *Canterbury*, who sent for *Thomas*,
and learnt of him the truth of it , whereupon he secretly determined in
his mind to make him his Successor.   But this Favour of the Virgin's in
the Present of a New Garment, was not so wonderful as another we are
told of,that concerned an Old one. For when he was Archbishop,he used
to wear a Hair-shirt next his Skin on Saturday, (a Day dedicated to the
Blessed Virgin) which being rent, *Wickman* tells us, that the Blessed
Virgin held his Shirt, whilst he stitched it ; but *Gonon* reports it thus.

Gonon.
Ibid.p 176.
& Wick-
man's Sab-
batismus
Maria-
nus, p. 73.

There was an English Priest that daily said the Mass of the Blessed Virgin,
because he had not skill to say any other; who being accused, was suspended
by St. Thomas from his Office for his want of skill. St. Thomas on a
time had hidden his Hair-shirt under his Bed, that at a convenient season he
might secretly sow it : The Blessed Virgin appeared to the foresaid Priest, and
commanded him to go to Thomas, *and tell him, that the Mother of God had*
granted leave to the Priest that daily celebrated her Mass, and was suspended,
to officiate again; by this token, that she, for whose love he said Mass, had
sowed his Hair-shirt that lay in such a place, and had left the Red Hair with
which she sowed it. Thomas hearing this, was amazed, and found it so
as the Priest related , and gave him power hereupon to officiate.

A Fowl is turn'd into a Carp for St. Thomas *his Conveniency.*

THE *English* Legend relates in the Life of St. *Thomas*, That when
 he was at *Rome*, upon a Fasting-day, a Fowl being provided for
his Dinner, because no Fish could be bought, the Capon was miraculously turned into a Carp, rather than the Holy Man should break the
Orders of the Church.

How God miraculously vindicated Thomas *against his Enemies in his Life-time.*

NOW St. *Thomas* being accounted the King's Enemy, began to be contemned, and hated by the common People, that coming to a Town called *Strode*, the Inhabitants of that Place meaning to put an affront upon this good Despised Father, presumed to cut off his Horses Tail which he rode upon : but hereby they brought a perpetual reproach upon themselves ; for afterwards it fell out, by the Pleasure of God, that all the Race of those Men that committed this Fact, were born with Tails, like Brute Beasts ; whence the Proverb comes of *Kentish Long-tails*. *Polyd. Virgil. Angli Hist. Lib. 13.*

The Wonderful Judgments of Thomas a Becket's *Murderers.*

ALL Men shunned their Company, and none eat or drank with them ; they cast the Fragments of their Meat to the Dogs, and when they had tasted them, they would eat no more of them : so manifest was God's Vengeance, that they who contemned the Lord's Anointed, were even contemned by Dogs. A Canoniz'd Historian adds further, That of those who killed him, some with their Teeth gnawed off their own Fingers in pieces, others had their Bodies flowing with Corrupt Matter, others were dissolved by the Palsy, and others miserably died of Madness. *Hoveden. Hist. p. 299. Antonin. Hist. To.2. p. 705.*

Certain Visions, Revelations and Miracles relating to St. Thomas a Becket's *Death.*

A Little before St. *Thomas* returned out of Banishment, it was revealed to him, that a few days after his return he should go to Heaven by dying a Martyr ; and we are told that while he was praying at the Monastery of *Pontiniac*, he heard a Voice from Heaven, saying, O Thomas, Thomas, *my Church shall be glorified in thy Blood.* A certain Young Man being under an Infirmity, his Soul went out of his Body, and returned again ; and he said he had been wrapt up into Heaven, and saw an empty Seat mightily adorned, placed among the Apostles ; And when he asked for whom that magnificent Seat was prepared, an Angel answered, it was reserved for a certain great Priest of the *English* Nation ; which was understood of St. *Thomas.* *Heraclius* also, the Patriarch of *Jerusalem*, coming into *England*, related this Vision. A certain Fryer was sick to Death in a Monastery of the Holy Land, the Abbot desired him to certify him of his state after Death, which he promised, and dyed. A few days after he appeared to the Abbot, and told him he enjoyed the Vision of God ; and that you may not doubt of my Happiness, know, saith he, *That when I was carried by Angels into Heaven,* *Antonin. Hist. To.2. p. 706. Harpsfield's Hist. Eccl. Angl. p. 334. Capgrave in the Life of St. Thomas, f. 292.*

there came a great Man with an unspeakable admirably Procession follow-ing him of Angels, Patriarchs, Prophets, and Apostles, &c. This Ma[n] stood before the Lord as a Martyr, all his Head being torn, and hi[s] Blood seeming to distil from the clefts of his Wounds. To whom the Lord said, O Thomas, *thus it becometh thee to enter into the Court of the Lord* ; and added, *I will give no less Glory to thee, than that I have bestowed on* Peter. *And the Lord took a mighty golden Crown, and put it on his Head.* The Fryer added, *Know for certain, that* Thomas *of* Canterbury *is slain about this time; mark my words, and observe the time :* And so he vanished. This the Abbot told to the Patriarch, who

Hoveden
Hist. p.
299. related it in *England.* Before St. *Thomas* was buried, as he lay in the Quire upon the Bier, in the morning, lifting up his Right Hand, he gave his Benediction to the Monks.

Cæsarius
Dialog.
dist. 8. c.
70. A certain Soldier, a great Lover of St. *Thomas,* was enquiring eve-ry where, How he might get any of his Reliques ? Which a crafty Priest hearing, at whose House he sojourned, said to him, I have by me a Bridle which St. *Thomas* long used ; which the Soldier hearing, gave him the Money he asked for it, and received the Bridle with much De-votion. And God, to whom nothing is impossible, willing to reward the Faith of the Soldier, vouchsafed to work many Miracles by that Bridle in Honour of his Martyr ; which the Soldier considering, built a Church in Honour of St. *Thomas,* and, instead of Reliques, put therein this Bridle of the cheating Priest.

Mighty Wonders performed in the Behalf of those that invoked St. Thomas's *help.*

Festiv. fol.
80.&c An-
toninus
loc. citat.
p. 707.
Lambert's
Peramb.of
Kent; p.
143. THere was a Bird, says the *Festivale,* that was taught to speak, and could say St. *Thomas* ; it hapned that this Bird sitting out of his Cage, a Spar-Hawk seiz'd on it, and was ready to kill it ; but the Bird crying, St. Thomas *help,* the Spar-Hawk fell down dead.

King *Lewis* of *France* was extraordinarily heard, for coming over to offer at this Saints Tomb at *Canterbury,* and praying for a safe Pas-sage, he obtained that neither he, nor any other from thenceforth that crossed the Seas between *Dover* and *Withsend,* should suffer any Loss or Shipwreck.

Antoni-
nus. Ibid. Again, A special Friend of *Thomas,* being under an Infirmity, came to the Tomb of the Saint, to pray for the recovery of his health, which he received to the full : But being return'd home, he thought within himself, that perhaps that Infirmity was inflicted on him for his Salva-tion, and was for the greater profit of his Soul than Health was ; and therefore returning to the Sepulchre of the Saint, he prayed, *That what should most conduce to his Salvation, whether Sickness or Health, that* Tho-mas *would obtain it for him of the Lord.* Whereupon his Infirmity re-turned again upon him.

St.

St. Thomas's *Civility to other Saints in the matter of Cures.*

A Clerk having been troubled with Vomiting, and a bloody Flux, and a Pain in his Eyes, that he was almoſt blind, he had for 15 days together implored the Martyrs help at *Canterbury* : to whom St. *Thomas* at laſt appeared, and bid him riſe quickly, and go to *Durrham* to St. *Cuthbert*, and by his Merits he ſhould obtain Mercy and Health: For (ſaid he) *I will have my languiſhing Patients and Servants go to him for Cure, and his come to me.* And the firſt day he came thither he was cured.

Capgr. vit. St. Cuthbert. fol. 78.

The peculiar Veneration paid to St. Thomas's *Shrine, even above that of the Bleſſed Virgin, or that of Jeſus Chriſt.*

WE are told of an Hundred thouſand People, that in ſome years, have come to pay their Devotions to his Shrine? Nay more, that their Zeal towards him was ſo hot, as ſometimes they ſeemed to have but little conſideration of the bleſſed Virgin her ſelf, and none at all of Chriſt. For there being three Altars in the Church of *Canterbury*, one dedicated to Chriſt, another to the Virgin *Mary*, and a third to *Thomas.* We are told out of an old Lieger-Book of that Church, that one Year the Offerings at the Shrine of *Thomas* amounted to 954 *l.* 6 *s.* 3 *d.* when thoſe to the bleſſed Virgin came only to 4 *l.* 1 *s.* 8 *d.* and to Chriſt nothing at all.

W. Sumner. Antiq. of Canter. p. 249. Cited by Foulis Hiſtory of Popiſh Treaſons, &c. p. 17.

Of a Man that had his Eyes put out, and his Privities cut off, and was made perfect again by St. Thomas.

ONE *Edwardus* having in his Drink broke into a Man's houſe, and ſtole ſome of his Goods, ſuch an Action of Felony was laid againſt him, that he was condemned to have his Eyes put out, and his Privities to be cut off, which Sentence was executed upon him ; and he being in danger of Death by bleeding, was counſelled to pray to St. *Thomas.* In the Night he had a Viſion of one in white Apparel, who bid him *watch and pray, and put his Truſt in God, and our Lady, and holy* St. Thomas. The next day the Man rubbing his Eyes, they were reſtored ; and a little after rubbing the other place, his *Pendenda*, (as he calls them) were alſo reſtored, very ſmall at the firſt, but growing ſtill greater, which he permitted every one to feel that would. No doubt the old *Roman* Breviary points at this Story, when it ſays thus : *Thomas ſtretched out his powerful hand to unuſual and unheard of Wonders : For even they that were deprived of their Eyes, and of thoſe parts by which Mankind is propagated*, by his Merits had the Favor to receive new ones.*

Brev. Roman. antiq. lect 9.

* Membris genitalibus privati.

The History of St. Patrick, and his Miracles.

Stani-
burst. ap.
Haræum.
17. Mart.

St. Beda.

Antiq.
Gluston.in
Patricio.
Horævas
in Patri-
cio.
Jocelin. in
vit. S. Pa-
tricii, c.
13.

In Antiq.
Glaston.in
Patricio.

St. Patrick, alias Socber, the great Apostle of Ireland, in A. D. 361. was born in the South-West Coast of Britany among the Dimetor in the Province called Pembrokeshire. His Father was Caliphurnius, a British Priest or Deacon; his Mother Concha, the Sister of St. Martin Bishop of Tours. The Village where he was born, was called Bannava, where anciently Gyants are said to have dwelt.

But Socber, afterwards called Patrick, was, in the Sixteenth year of his Age, led away Captive in an Incursion made by the Picts into England, and sold to a Noble-man in the Northern parts of Ireland. Six whole Years the devout Youth spent in this slavery, all the while addressing his Prayers to God an hundred times aday, and as oft in the night, using great Mortification likewise; so that with these two wings he mounted to such Perfection, as he enjoy'd a frequent Conversation with Angels. And particularly in Capgrave, we read how an Angel, called Victor, frequently visited him, and said to him, Thou dost very well to fast, ere long thou shalt return to thy Countrey. But after six Years slavery, St. Patrick, by the admonition of an Angel, found under a certain Turf a Sum of Gold, which he gave to his Lord, and so was delivered from Captivity, and returned to his Parents Countrey, which he gloriously illustrated with the admirable Sanctity of his Life.

Staniburst
in vit.
S. Patric.

Afterwards repairing to Rome, he received his Mission for the Conversion of Ireland, from Pope Celestinus, who changed his Name to Patricius, as prophecying he should be the spiritual Father of many Souls, and so was promoted to his Episcopal Dignity, and directed to his Voyage into Ireland; and at the same time received of the Pope twelve Years of Indulgence.

ap. Cap-
grav. in S.
Patricio.

The Irish Magicians gave this warning of St. Patrick's coming into Ireland several Years before, saying, A Man will come hither with his Wood, whose Table shall be placed on the Eastern side of his House, and some persons standing behind, together with the other, from the Table will sing, and the Congregation will answer them, saying, Amen. When this Man comes he will destroy our Gods, subvert our Temples, destroy Princes which resist him, and his Doctrine shall remain and prevail here for ever.

Jocelin. in
vit. S. Pa-
tricii, c.
26.

Now the piece of Wood foretold by those Magicians, is interpreted a certain wonderful Staff which St. Patrick, before his Journey, received from an Holy Hermit, and which was called, The Staff of Jesus. Now

St. *Patrick* by Divine Revelation pass'd over to a certain solitary Hermit living in an Island of the *Tyrrhen* Sea, whose name was *Justus*, which he made good by his Actions, being a Man of a Holy Life, great fame, and much merit. After devout Salutations and good Discourse, the same Man of God gave to St. *Patrick* a Staff, which he seriously affirmed had been bestowed on him immediately by the hand of our Lord *Jesus* himself, who had appeared to him.

Now there were in the same Island at some distance other Men also who liv'd solitary Lives: Of which some seem'd very fresh and youthful, others were decrepid old Men. St. *Patrick* after some conversation with them, was informed that those very old Men were Children to those who appeared so youthful. At which being astonish'd and enquiring the occasion of so great a Miracle, they thus acquainted him, saying, *We from our Childhood by Divine Grace have been much addicted to Works of Mercy, so that our Doors were always open to all Travellers which demand Meat or Lodging. On a certain Night it hapned that a Stranger, having a Staff in his hand, was entertain'd by us, whom we used with all the Courtefie we could. On the Morning after he gave us his Benediction, and said, I am* Jesus Christ: *My Members you have hitherto oft ministred to, and this Night entertain'd me in my own Person. After this he gave the Staff which he had in his hand to a Man of God, our Father both spiritually and carnally, commanding him to keep it, till in succeeding times a certain Stranger, named* Patrick, *should come to visit him: and to him he should give it. Having said this, he presently ascended into Heaven. And from that day we have remained in the same state of youthful Comliness and Vigour to this hour. Whereas our Children, who then were little Infants, are now, as you see, become decrepid old Men.* Farther, in the vulgar Opinion with this Staff St. *Patrick* cast out of the Island all Venomous Beasts.

St. *Patrick* landed in the Province of *Lenster* in the Year 432. where having converted *Sinel* the Son of *Finchado*, he directed his Journey into *Ulster*, where one *Dicon* coming suddenly with Weapons, intended to kill the Saint and his Companions. But as soon as he saw the Holy Bishop's face, he felt compunction in his heart, led the Saint to his House, had the Faith of *Christ* preacht to him, and was converted.

While St. *Patrick* remain'd in *Ireland*, the Holy Son of God shew'd Man Reve-

Girald. Cambrensi in topographi. l. 34.

Capgrave
in Patric.
Jocelin *in*
Patricio.

Antic.
Glaston *in*
Patricio.
Gul.
Malmsbu.
Avam de
Domer-
ham. Joan.
Mona-
chus.

After eight years labouring in our Lord's Vineyard in *Ireland,* to the Conversion of that Island, St. *Patrick* return'd to *Britany,* and so went on to *Rome,* there to give an Account of his Apostleship. At his return thence to his Native Countrey, he retired to *Glastenbury,* where he foretold with the Tongue and Spirit of Prophecy many unfortunate, and many prosperous things which in future times should befall *Britany;* and moreover foresaw and foretold the Sanctity of St. *David* who was in his Mother's Womb. And at last yielded to Nature in the thirty ninth year after his return to the said Island, and was buried in the Old Church on the Right hand of the Altar by direction of an Angel, a great flame likewise in the sight of all breaking forth in the same place. He lived one hundred and eleven years.

Certain Saints that performed Wonderful Conversions.

Colganus
ad 6 Feb
in ....chi
p. 269.

Such. entertained St. *Ædus* the Bishop, and set a great Supper of Flesh before him, but the Bishop would not eat Flesh, but blessing the Meat, it was turned into Bread, and Fish, and Honey. And in the Life of St. *Moedoc* we are told, That when St. *Molua* had killed a fat Calf for to receive him, hearing that St. *Moedoc* did not eat Flesh, he blessed eight pieces of Flesh, and they became eight Fishes; but the Bi-shop knowing by Inspiration how they were made Fishes, he blessed

Colganus
Act. Sanct.
Hibern. *ad*
Jac. 31.
p. 281.

them again, and they were turned again into eight pieces of Flesh; which St. *Malua* seeing, he was displeased; for he had no other Fishes in his Monastery, and therefore before them all, he blessed them again, and they became right Fishes the second time, and here the Contest ceased; and for the Honour of St. *Molua,* he was contented to feed upon them.

F I N I S.